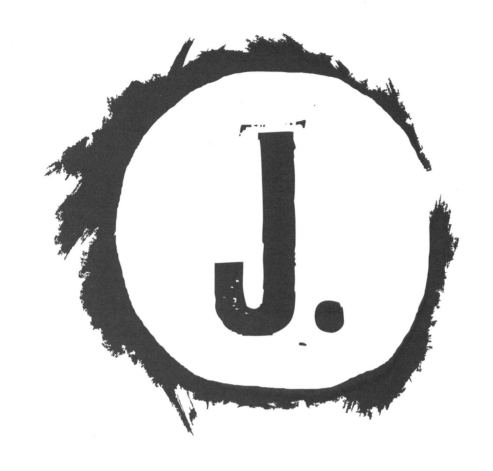

JESUS-CENTERED

Planner

2020

DISCOVERING MY PURPOSE
WITH JESUS EVERY DAY

Jesus-Centered Planner 2020
Discovering My Purpose With Jesus Every Day

Copyright © 2019 Group Publishing, Inc./0000 0001 0362 4853
Lifetree™ is an imprint of Group Publishing, Inc.
Visit our websites: **MyLifetree.com** and **group.com**

Credits
Author: Jeff White
Chief Creative Officer: Joani Schultz
Editor: Cherie Shifflett
Assistant Editor: Lyndsay Gerwing
Art Director: Jeff Storm
Production and Cover Art: Darrin Stoll
Production Manager: Melissa Towers

Scripture quotations are taken from the Holy Bible, New Living Translation, copyright ©1996, 2004, 2015 by Tyndale House Foundation. Used by permission of Tyndale House Publishers, Inc., Carol Stream, Illinois 60188. All rights reserved.

ISBN: 978-1-4707-5962-9
Printed in China.

10 9 8 7 6 5 4 3 2 1   28 27 26 25 24 23 22 21 20 19

Welcome to the JESUS-CENTERED (J.) Planner

Dear Jesus-follower,

For many people, 2020 is a year of focus. We have a constant reminder with the date itself (the obvious 20/20 vision reference) to keep our eyes on Jesus every day of the year.

You often hear people ask, "What would Jesus do?" But when it comes to our daily lives, there's a better question we should be asking: "What *did* Jesus do?" The answers can be very helpful in prioritizing your vision of the year ahead and planning your schedule in a way that keeps you attached to the heart of Jesus.

In the weekly devotional prompts, you'll discover how focusing on Jesus' real-life experiences can guide your own personal goals and plans. And the daily Scripture readings will lead you through the life of Jesus, so you can see for yourself what Jesus considered most important.

It's all about staying centered on Jesus in ways that are both meaningful and practical. So enjoy the journey! And see how centering your life on Jesus will bring your vision into the sharpest clarity and focus possible.

2020

January
S	M	T	W	T	F	S
		1	2	3	4	
5	6	7	8	9	10	11
12	13	14	15	16	17	18
19	20	21	22	23	24	25
26	27	28	29	30	31	

February
S	M	T	W	T	F	S
						1
2	3	4	5	6	7	8
9	10	11	12	13	14	15
16	17	18	19	20	21	22
23	24	25	26	27	28	29

March
S	M	T	W	T	F	S
1	2	3	4	5	6	7
8	9	10	11	12	13	14
15	16	17	18	19	20	21
22	23	24	25	26	27	28
29	30	31				

April
S	M	T	W	T	F	S
			1	2	3	4
5	6	7	8	9	10	11
12	13	14	15	16	17	18
19	20	21	22	23	24	25
26	27	28	29	30		

May
S	M	T	W	T	F	S
					1	2
3	4	5	6	7	8	9
10	11	12	13	14	15	16
17	18	19	20	21	22	23
24	25	26	27	28	29	30
31						

June
S	M	T	W	T	F	S
	1	2	3	4	5	6
7	8	9	10	11	12	13
14	15	16	17	18	19	20
21	22	23	24	25	26	27
28	29	30				

July
S	M	T	W	T	F	S
			1	2	3	4
5	6	7	8	9	10	11
12	13	14	15	16	17	18
19	20	21	22	23	24	25
26	27	28	29	30	31	

August
S	M	T	W	T	F	S
						1
2	3	4	5	6	7	8
9	10	11	12	13	14	15
16	17	18	19	20	21	22
23	24	25	26	27	28	29
30	31					

September
S	M	T	W	T	F	S
		1	2	3	4	5
6	7	8	9	10	11	12
13	14	15	16	17	18	19
20	21	22	23	24	25	26
27	28	29	30			

October
S	M	T	W	T	F	S
				1	2	3
4	5	6	7	8	9	10
11	12	13	14	15	16	17
18	19	20	21	22	23	24
25	26	27	28	29	30	31

November
S	M	T	W	T	F	S
1	2	3	4	5	6	7
8	9	10	11	12	13	14
15	16	17	18	19	20	21
22	23	24	25	26	27	28
29	30					

December
S	M	T	W	T	F	S
		1	2	3	4	5
6	7	8	9	10	11	12
13	14	15	16	17	18	19
20	21	22	23	24	25	26
27	28	29	30	31		

U.S. Holidays

Jan 1	New Year's Day
Jan 20	Martin Luther King Jr. Day
Feb 14	Valentine's Day
Feb 17	Presidents Day
Apr 10	Good Friday
Apr 12	Easter Sunday
May 10	Mother's Day
May 25	Memorial Day
Jun 21	Father's Day
Jul 4	Independence Day
Sep 7	Labor Day
Oct 12	Columbus Day
Oct 31	Halloween
Nov 11	Veterans Day
Nov 26	Thanksgiving Day
Dec 24	Christmas Eve
Dec 25	Christmas Day
Dec 31	New Year's Eve

2021

January

S	M	T	W	T	F	S
					1	2
3	4	5	6	7	8	9
10	11	12	13	14	15	16
17	18	19	20	21	22	23
24	25	26	27	28	29	30
31						

February

S	M	T	W	T	F	S
	1	2	3	4	5	6
7	8	9	10	11	12	13
14	15	16	17	18	19	20
21	22	23	24	25	26	27
28						

March

S	M	T	W	T	F	S
	1	2	3	4	5	6
7	8	9	10	11	12	13
14	15	16	17	18	19	20
21	22	23	24	25	26	27
28	29	30	31			

April

S	M	T	W	T	F	S
				1	2	3
4	5	6	7	8	9	10
11	12	13	14	15	16	17
18	19	20	21	22	23	24
25	26	27	28	29	30	

May

S	M	T	W	T	F	S
						1
2	3	4	5	6	7	8
9	10	11	12	13	14	15
16	17	18	19	20	21	22
23	24	25	26	27	28	29
30	31					

June

S	M	T	W	T	F	S
		1	2	3	4	5
6	7	8	9	10	11	12
13	14	15	16	17	18	19
20	21	22	23	24	25	26
27	28	29	30			

July

S	M	T	W	T	F	S
				1	2	3
4	5	6	7	8	9	10
11	12	13	14	15	16	17
18	19	20	21	22	23	24
25	26	27	28	29	30	31

August

S	M	T	W	T	F	S
1	2	3	4	5	6	7
8	9	10	11	12	13	14
15	16	17	18	19	20	21
22	23	24	25	26	27	28
29	30	31				

September

S	M	T	W	T	F	S
			1	2	3	4
5	6	7	8	9	10	11
12	13	14	15	16	17	18
19	20	21	22	23	24	25
26	27	28	29	30		

October

S	M	T	W	T	F	S
					1	2
3	4	5	6	7	8	9
10	11	12	13	14	15	16
17	18	19	20	21	22	23
24	25	26	27	28	29	30
31						

November

S	M	T	W	T	F	S
	1	2	3	4	5	6
7	8	9	10	11	12	13
14	15	16	17	18	19	20
21	22	23	24	25	26	27
28	29	30				

December

S	M	T	W	T	F	S
		1	2	3	4
5	6	7	8	9	10	11
12	13	14	15	16	17	18
19	20	21	22	23	24	25
26	27	28	29	30	31	

U.S. Holidays

Jan 1	New Year's Day
Jan 18	Martin Luther King Jr. Day
Feb 14	Valentine's Day
Feb 15	Presidents Day
Apr 2	Good Friday
Apr 4	Easter Sunday
May 9	Mother's Day
May 31	Memorial Day
Jun 20	Father's Day
Jul 4	Independence Day
Sep 6	Labor Day
Oct 11	Columbus Day
Oct 31	Halloween
Nov 11	Veterans Day
Nov 25	Thanksgiving Day
Dec 24	Christmas Eve
Dec 25	Christmas Day
Dec 31	New Year's Eve

How to Use This Planner

The *Jesus-Centered Planner* is designed to help you partner with Jesus to accomplish goals and organize your days with his mission as your guide. Here's how the planner works.

Goal Setting

Goal-setting worksheets invite Jesus into your goal-setting process and help you maintain your focus on Jesus in the midst of your busy life. To keep the process manageable, we've limited your goals to a three-month timeline. This means you'll have an opportunity to choose new goals each quarter, either building on the previous quarter's goals or starting fresh with the new things Jesus has put on your heart.

REMINDER: Use a pencil for this section, and limit yourself to a maximum of three goals.

With Jesus' command in mind, prayerfully consider one to three goals you can set for yourself for this quarter.

QUARTERLY GOAL (JANUARY, FEBRUARY, MARCH)

Achieving this goal is important to you because…

Tips for Goal Setting

Use a pencil. This eliminates the pressure of getting your goals perfectly right and gives you the flexibility to tweak them (or change them completely) each week.

Limit yourself to three goals per quarter. Don't bite off more than you can chew. Every new goal you add divides your focus, so pray about how many goals Jesus has for you each quarter, and don't tackle more than three at a time.

Monthly Calendar

To Do

JANUARY 2020

	Sunday	Monday	Tuesday		Wednesday	Thursday	Friday	Saturday
	29	30	31		1 New Year's Day	2	3	4
	5	6	7		8	9	10	11
	12	13	14		15	16	17	18
	19	20	21		22	23	24	25
Notes	26	27 Martin Luther King Jr. Day	28		29	30	31	1

This month, focus on Jesus by...

Loving others: Who are you going to be intentional about showing love to this month? Write their names here, and schedule time to connect with them.

Use your monthly calendar to ensure that your priorities align with Jesus'.

This calendar prompts you to identify at least one way to focus on Jesus each month. It also prompts you to check in with Jesus to discover who he wants you to connect with each month.

This month, focus on Jesus by...

Loving others: Who are you going to be intentional about showing love to this month? Write their names here, and schedule time to connect with them.

Weekly Schedule

29 Sunday	30 Monday	31 Tuesday	1 Wednesday		2 Thursday	3 Friday	4 Saturday	What do you need to pray about this week?
READ Revelation 20	READ Revelation 21	READ Revelation 22	READ Matthew 1		READ Matthew 2	READ Matthew 3	READ Matthew 4	
6:00	6:00	6:00	6:00		6:00	6:00	6:00	
7:00	7:00	7:00	7:00		7:00	7:00	7:00	
8:00	8:00	8:00	8:00		8:00	8:00	8:00	
9:00	9:00	9:00	9:00		9:00	9:00	9:00	
10:00	10:00	10:00	10:00		10:00	10:00	10:00	
11:00	11:00	11:00	11:00		11:00	11:00	11:00	
12:00	12:00	12:00	12:00		12:00	12:00	12:00	
1:00	1:00	1:00	1:00		1:00	1:00	1:00	
2:00	2:00	2:00	2:00		2:00	2:00	2:00	
3:00	3:00	3:00	3:00		3:00	3:00	3:00	To Do
4:00	4:00	4:00	4:00		4:00	4:00	4:00	
5:00	5:00	5:00	5:00		5:00	5:00	5:00	
6:00	6:00	6:00	6:00		6:00	6:00	6:00	
7:00	7:00	7:00	7:00		7:00	7:00	7:00	
8:00	8:00	8:00	8:00		8:00	8:00	8:00	
9:00	9:00	9:00	9:00		9:00	9:00	9:00	
10:00	10:00	10:00	10:00		10:00	10:00	10:00	

Things you're thankful for this week:

J. *The new year brings a chance for a fresh start. Letting Jesus be the center of your life may mean changing your daily habits. What's one routine you will need to adjust to allow Jesus to be more of a focus?*

The weekly schedule is going to be the primary part of this book that helps you stay centered on Jesus. These four features are designed to help you keep your vision for the year in focus:

- *Jesus-centered devotional prompt:* Every week you'll find a creative new way to stay attached to Jesus and keep him at your center every day.

- *Gratitude prompt:* Record the things you're most grateful for each week, and give thanks to Jesus for each one.

- *Prayer prompt:* Take time to talk to Jesus every week.

- *Jesus-centered daily Bible-reading plan:* Spend time every day with a Bible chapter that gives you a fresh perspective on the life and teachings of Jesus. Use the *Jesus-Centered Bible*, which features Jesus connections from Genesis to Revelation, to get the most out of your daily reading time.

The new year brings a chance for a fresh start. Letting Jesus be the center of your life may mean changing your daily habits. What's one routine you will need to adjust to allow Jesus to be more of a focus?

- **Jesus-centered devotional prompt**
- **Gratitude prompt**
- **Prayer prompt**
- **Jesus-centered daily Bible-reading plan**

Things you're thankful for this week:

What do you need to pray about this week?

WEEK 1
DEC 29 – JAN 4

29 Sunday

READ
Revelation 20

6:00

7:00

8:00

30 Monday

READ
Revelation 21

6:00

7:00

8:00

Monthly Reflections

Review your gratitude notes from the previous weeks, and write a prayer to Jesus thanking him for this month.

Reviewing the previous month, how have you grown?

What is an area or two in which you'd like to continue to grow?

What experiences, insights, and moments kept you centered on Jesus this month? Record them here so you don't forget them.

Review your appointments and tasks for the coming month. How are they aligned with Jesus' command to love others? Is there anything you need to cancel, add, or change? Pray about it; then update your schedule as needed.

Now write a prayer thanking Jesus for the month ahead, and include one way you're planning to stay focused on him.

At the end of each month, you'll have an opportunity to recall what you've learned and reflect on how Jesus is affecting your life. Through a series of questions, you'll review goals, celebrate accomplishments, and look forward to each new month.

Blank Pages

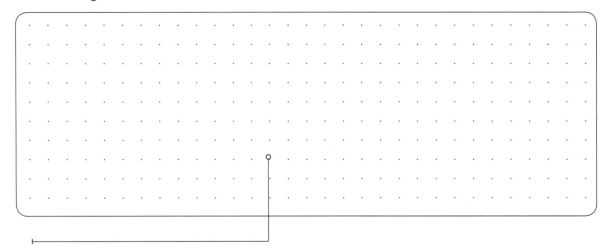

You'll find blank pages at the back of your planner. Use them for lists, tracking projects, journaling, prayers, doodling—whatever you like.

A Word About Being Jesus-Centered

What does it really mean to be "centered on Jesus"? This planner is designed for people who believe their lives can be richer, more joyful, and more meaningful when they make Jesus the hub of their existence.

So how do you make Jesus the center?

We begin with the words of Jesus taken from John 15: "I am the vine; you are the branches. Those who remain in me, and I in them, will produce much fruit. For apart from me you can do nothing" (John 15:5). Being Jesus-centered means staying *attached* to Jesus, just like a branch stays attached to the vine.

So how do you stay attached?

Jesus explains: "When you obey my commandments, you remain in my love... This is my commandment: Love each other in the same way I have loved you" (John 15:10, 12). The key to staying attached to the Vine is to love others. You cannot be Jesus-centered if you aren't focused on loving others.

So how do you love others?

The Bible describes that for us in detail in 1 Corinthians 13:4-7: "Love is patient and kind. Love is not jealous or boastful or proud or rude. It does not demand its own way. It is not irritable, and it keeps no record of being wronged. It does not rejoice about injustice but rejoices whenever the truth wins out. Love never gives up, never loses faith, is always hopeful, and endures through every circumstance."

This year's focus on being Jesus-centered pays a lot of attention to that one all-important command of Jesus. You'll find your life truly focused on Jesus when you're putting his love into action through your daily life. This planner will help you do just that.

Setting Jesus-Centered Goals, First Quarter

Look to Jesus' example to guide you during your goal-setting.

Before committing to goals, spend 5 to 10 minutes writing or mapping a sketch of everything that's currently on your heart relating to your dreams and aspirations. Don't edit yourself; it's okay if this list includes your most personal desires or things that seem impossible. Be open and honest with yourself about where your heart is right now.

Now think about Jesus' command to love others. How are Jesus' words connected to your own dreams and aspirations? Pray about it. Challenge yourself to be open to what that really means for you. If staying attached to Jesus is all about loving others, how will that affect your goals? If needed, rework your goals here.

With Jesus' command in mind, prayerfully consider one to three goals you can set for yourself for this quarter.

QUARTERLY GOAL (JANUARY, FEBRUARY, MARCH)

Achieving this goal is important to you because...

Achieving this goal is important to Jesus because...

ACTION STEPS needed to accomplish this goal...

If you've identified one or two other quarterly goals, write them here along with the reasons they're important and the action steps you'll take to achieve them.

JANUARY 2020

Sunday	Monday	Tuesday
29	30	31
5	6	7
12	13	14
19	20 Martin Luther King Jr. Day	21
26	27	28

Notes

This month, focus on Jesus by...

Wednesday	Thursday	Friday	Saturday
1 New Year's Day	2	3	4
8	9	10	11
15	16	17	18
22	23	24	25
29	30	31	1

Loving others: Who are you going to be intentional about showing love to this month? Write their names here, and schedule time to connect with them.

29 Sunday

READ
Revelation 20

6:00

7:00

8:00

9:00

10:00

11:00

12:00

1:00

2:00

3:00

4:00

5:00

6:00

7:00

8:00

9:00

10:00

30 Monday

READ
Revelation 21

6:00

7:00

8:00

9:00

10:00

11:00

12:00

1:00

2:00

3:00

4:00

5:00

6:00

7:00

8:00

9:00

10:00

31 Tuesday

READ
Revelation 22

6:00

7:00

8:00

9:00

10:00

11:00

12:00

1:00

2:00

3:00

4:00

5:00

6:00

7:00

8:00

9:00

10:00

1   Wednesday

READ
Matthew 1

6:00

7:00

8:00

9:00

10:00

11:00

12:00

1:00

2:00

3:00

4:00

5:00

6:00

7:00

8:00

9:00

10:00

The new year brings a chance for a fresh start. Letting Jesus be the center of your life may mean changing your daily habits. What's one routine you will need to adjust to allow Jesus to be more of a focus?

2 Thursday

READ
Matthew 2

6:00

7:00

8:00

9:00

10:00

11:00

12:00

1:00

2:00

3:00

4:00

5:00

6:00

7:00

8:00

9:00

10:00

3 Friday

READ
Matthew 3

6:00

7:00

8:00

9:00

10:00

11:00

12:00

1:00

2:00

3:00

4:00

5:00

6:00

7:00

8:00

9:00

10:00

4 Saturday

READ
Matthew 4

6:00

7:00

8:00

9:00

10:00

11:00

12:00

1:00

2:00

3:00

4:00

5:00

6:00

7:00

8:00

9:00

10:00

What do you need to pray about this week?

To Do

Things you're thankful for this week:

5 Sunday
READ
Matthew 5:1-26

6:00
7:00
8:00
9:00
10:00
11:00
12:00
1:00
2:00
3:00
4:00
5:00
6:00
7:00
8:00
9:00
10:00

6 Monday
READ
Matthew 5:27-48

6:00
7:00
8:00
9:00
10:00
11:00
12:00
1:00
2:00
3:00
4:00
5:00
6:00
7:00
8:00
9:00
10:00

7 Tuesday
READ
Matthew 6:1-18

6:00
7:00
8:00
9:00
10:00
11:00
12:00
1:00
2:00
3:00
4:00
5:00
6:00
7:00
8:00
9:00
10:00

8 Wednesday
READ
Matthew 6:19-34

6:00
7:00
8:00
9:00
10:00
11:00
12:00
1:00
2:00
3:00
4:00
5:00
6:00
7:00
8:00
9:00
10:00

As you orbit your daily life around Jesus, it's helpful to remember that you're not starting entirely from scratch. Think of two or three ways you've kept Jesus close in recent months.

9 Thursday

READ
Matthew 7

6:00

7:00

8:00

9:00

10:00

11:00

12:00

1:00

2:00

3:00

4:00

5:00

6:00

7:00

8:00

9:00

10:00

10 Friday

READ
Matthew 8:1-17

6:00

7:00

8:00

9:00

10:00

11:00

12:00

1:00

2:00

3:00

4:00

5:00

6:00

7:00

8:00

9:00

10:00

11 Saturday

READ
Matthew 8:18-34

6:00

7:00

8:00

9:00

10:00

11:00

12:00

1:00

2:00

3:00

4:00

5:00

6:00

7:00

8:00

9:00

10:00

What do you need to pray about this week?

To Do

Things you're thankful for this week:

12 Sunday

READ
Matthew 9:1-17

6:00

7:00

8:00

9:00

10:00

11:00

12:00

1:00

2:00

3:00

4:00

5:00

6:00

7:00

8:00

9:00

10:00

13 Monday

READ
Matthew 9:18-38

6:00

7:00

8:00

9:00

10:00

11:00

12:00

1:00

2:00

3:00

4:00

5:00

6:00

7:00

8:00

9:00

10:00

14 Tuesday

READ
Matthew 10:1-20

6:00

7:00

8:00

9:00

10:00

11:00

12:00

1:00

2:00

3:00

4:00

5:00

6:00

7:00

8:00

9:00

10:00

15 Wednesday

READ
Matthew 10:21-42

6:00

7:00

8:00

9:00

10:00

11:00

12:00

1:00

2:00

3:00

4:00

5:00

6:00

7:00

8:00

9:00

10:00

Loving others—Jesus' top command—involves you pouring Jesus' love into someone else's life. Be sure to set aside time in your calendar to do one kind thing for someone you know. As you do, you're keeping Jesus at the center of your life.

16 Thursday

READ
Matthew 11

6:00

7:00

8:00

9:00

10:00

11:00

12:00

1:00

2:00

3:00

4:00

5:00

6:00

7:00

8:00

9:00

10:00

17 Friday

READ
Matthew 12:1-23

6:00

7:00

8:00

9:00

10:00

11:00

12:00

1:00

2:00

3:00

4:00

5:00

6:00

7:00

8:00

9:00

10:00

18 Saturday

READ
Matthew 12:24-50

6:00

7:00

8:00

9:00

10:00

11:00

12:00

1:00

2:00

3:00

4:00

5:00

6:00

7:00

8:00

9:00

10:00

What do you need to pray about this week?

To Do

Things you're thankful for this week:

19 Sunday	*20 Monday*	*21 Tuesday*	*22 Wednesday*
READ *Matthew 13:1-30*	READ *Matthew 13:31-58*	READ *Matthew 14:1-21*	READ *Matthew 14:22-36*
6:00	6:00	6:00	6:00
7:00	7:00	7:00	7:00
8:00	8:00	8:00	8:00
9:00	9:00	9:00	9:00
10:00	10:00	10:00	10:00
11:00	11:00	11:00	11:00
12:00	12:00	12:00	12:00
1:00	1:00	1:00	1:00
2:00	2:00	2:00	2:00
3:00	3:00	3:00	3:00
4:00	4:00	4:00	4:00
5:00	5:00	5:00	5:00
6:00	6:00	6:00	6:00
7:00	7:00	7:00	7:00
8:00	8:00	8:00	8:00
9:00	9:00	9:00	9:00
10:00	10:00	10:00	10:00

*Gratitude is a key element in this **Jesus-Centered Planner**, as it helps you be mindful of all that God is doing in your life. Take a moment every week to write at least one thing you're thankful that Jesus brings into your life.*

23 Thursday

READ
Matthew 15:1-20

6:00

7:00

8:00

9:00

10:00

11:00

12:00

1:00

2:00

3:00

4:00

5:00

6:00

7:00

8:00

9:00

10:00

24 Friday

READ
Matthew 15:21-39

6:00

7:00

8:00

9:00

10:00

11:00

12:00

1:00

2:00

3:00

4:00

5:00

6:00

7:00

8:00

9:00

10:00

25 Saturday

READ
Matthew 16

6:00

7:00

8:00

9:00

10:00

11:00

12:00

1:00

2:00

3:00

4:00

5:00

6:00

7:00

8:00

9:00

10:00

What do you need to pray about this week?

To Do

Things you're thankful for this week:

26 Sunday

READ
Matthew 17

6:00

7:00

8:00

9:00

10:00

11:00

12:00

1:00

2:00

3:00

4:00

5:00

6:00

7:00

8:00

9:00

10:00

27 Monday

READ
Matthew 18:1-20

6:00

7:00

8:00

9:00

10:00

11:00

12:00

1:00

2:00

3:00

4:00

5:00

6:00

7:00

8:00

9:00

10:00

28 Tuesday

READ
Matthew 18:21-35

6:00

7:00

8:00

9:00

10:00

11:00

12:00

1:00

2:00

3:00

4:00

5:00

6:00

7:00

8:00

9:00

10:00

29 Wednesday

READ
Matthew 19

6:00

7:00

8:00

9:00

10:00

11:00

12:00

1:00

2:00

3:00

4:00

5:00

6:00

7:00

8:00

9:00

10:00

As you keep yourself (the branch) attached to Jesus (the vine), you may be producing "fruit" in your life. Which of these spiritual fruits have you experienced so far this year: love, joy, peace, patience, kindness, goodness, faithfulness, gentleness, or self-control?

30 Thursday

READ
Matthew 20:1-16

6:00

7:00

8:00

9:00

10:00

11:00

12:00

1:00

2:00

3:00

4:00

5:00

6:00

7:00

8:00

9:00

10:00

31 Friday

READ
Matthew 20:17-34

6:00

7:00

8:00

9:00

10:00

11:00

12:00

1:00

2:00

3:00

4:00

5:00

6:00

7:00

8:00

9:00

10:00

1 Saturday

READ
Matthew 21:1-22

6:00

7:00

8:00

9:00

10:00

11:00

12:00

1:00

2:00

3:00

4:00

5:00

6:00

7:00

8:00

9:00

10:00

What do you need to pray about this week?

To Do

Things you're thankful for this week:

Review your gratitude notes from the previous weeks, and write a prayer to Jesus thanking him for this month.

What experiences, insights, and moments kept you centered on Jesus this month? Record them here so you don't forget them.

Reviewing the previous month, how have you grown?

What is an area or two in which you'd like to continue to grow?

Review your appointments and tasks for the coming month. How are they aligned with Jesus' command to love others? Is there anything you need to cancel, add, or change? Pray about it; then update your schedule as needed.

Now write a prayer thanking Jesus for the month ahead, and include one way you're planning to stay focused on him.

FEBRUARY 2020

Sunday	Monday	Tuesday
26	27	28
2	3	4
9	10	11
16	17	18
23	24	25

Notes

This month, focus on Jesus by...

Wednesday	Thursday	Friday	Saturday
29	30	31	1
5	6	7	8
12	13	14 Valentine's Day	15
19	20	21	22
26	27	28	29

Loving others: Who are you going to be intentional about showing love to this month? Write their names here, and schedule time to connect with them.

2 Sunday

READ
Matthew 21:23-46

6:00

7:00

8:00

9:00

10:00

11:00

12:00

1:00

2:00

3:00

4:00

5:00

6:00

7:00

8:00

9:00

10:00

3 Monday

READ
Matthew 22:1-22

6:00

7:00

8:00

9:00

10:00

11:00

12:00

1:00

2:00

3:00

4:00

5:00

6:00

7:00

8:00

9:00

10:00

4 Tuesday

READ
Matthew 22:23-46

6:00

7:00

8:00

9:00

10:00

11:00

12:00

1:00

2:00

3:00

4:00

5:00

6:00

7:00

8:00

9:00

10:00

5 Wednesday

READ
Matthew 23:1-22

6:00

7:00

8:00

9:00

10:00

11:00

12:00

1:00

2:00

3:00

4:00

5:00

6:00

7:00

8:00

9:00

10:00

Are you making prayer a part of your daily life? Prayer is simply talking with Jesus, just like you would talk with a friend sitting next to you. If it helps, make a note in your planner to spend a few minutes telling Jesus about your day.

6 Thursday

READ
Matthew 23:23-39

6:00

7:00

8:00

9:00

10:00

11:00

12:00

1:00

2:00

3:00

4:00

5:00

6:00

7:00

8:00

9:00

10:00

7 Friday

READ
Matthew 24:1-28

6:00

7:00

8:00

9:00

10:00

11:00

12:00

1:00

2:00

3:00

4:00

5:00

6:00

7:00

8:00

9:00

10:00

8 Saturday

READ
Matthew 24:29-51

6:00

7:00

8:00

9:00

10:00

11:00

12:00

1:00

2:00

3:00

4:00

5:00

6:00

7:00

8:00

9:00

10:00

What do you need to pray about this week?

To Do

Things you're thankful for this week:

9 Sunday

READ
Matthew 25:1-30

6:00

7:00

8:00

9:00

10:00

11:00

12:00

1:00

2:00

3:00

4:00

5:00

6:00

7:00

8:00

9:00

10:00

10 Monday

READ
Matthew 25:31-46

6:00

7:00

8:00

9:00

10:00

11:00

12:00

1:00

2:00

3:00

4:00

5:00

6:00

7:00

8:00

9:00

10:00

11 Tuesday

READ
Matthew 26:1-25

6:00

7:00

8:00

9:00

10:00

11:00

12:00

1:00

2:00

3:00

4:00

5:00

6:00

7:00

8:00

9:00

10:00

12 Wednesday

READ
Matthew 26:26-50

6:00

7:00

8:00

9:00

10:00

11:00

12:00

1:00

2:00

3:00

4:00

5:00

6:00

7:00

8:00

9:00

10:00

God created the concept of the Sabbath as a time to rest, recharge, and focus on God. Since this is the seventh week of the year, schedule some time for yourself to let go of work, chores, and other stresses to rest in Jesus.

13 Thursday

READ
Matthew 26:51-75

6:00

7:00

8:00

9:00

10:00

11:00

12:00

1:00

2:00

3:00

4:00

5:00

6:00

7:00

8:00

9:00

10:00

14 Friday

READ
Matthew 27:1-26

6:00

7:00

8:00

9:00

10:00

11:00

12:00

1:00

2:00

3:00

4:00

5:00

6:00

7:00

8:00

9:00

10:00

15 Saturday

READ
Matthew 27:27-50

6:00

7:00

8:00

9:00

10:00

11:00

12:00

1:00

2:00

3:00

4:00

5:00

6:00

7:00

8:00

9:00

10:00

What do you need to pray about this week?

To Do

Things you're thankful for this week:

16 Sunday
READ
Matthew 27:51-66

6:00

7:00

8:00

9:00

10:00

11:00

12:00

1:00

2:00

3:00

4:00

5:00

6:00

7:00

8:00

9:00

10:00

17 Monday
READ
Matthew 28

6:00

7:00

8:00

9:00

10:00

11:00

12:00

1:00

2:00

3:00

4:00

5:00

6:00

7:00

8:00

9:00

10:00

18 Tuesday
READ
Mark 1:1-22

6:00

7:00

8:00

9:00

10:00

11:00

12:00

1:00

2:00

3:00

4:00

5:00

6:00

7:00

8:00

9:00

10:00

19 Wednesday
READ
Mark 1:23-45

6:00

7:00

8:00

9:00

10:00

11:00

12:00

1:00

2:00

3:00

4:00

5:00

6:00

7:00

8:00

9:00

10:00

Some people say talking with Jesus is like chatting with a friend, while others admit it feels like interacting with an imaginary friend. You can always listen to Jesus by reading his words in the Bible. Take advantage of the daily readings in your planner.

20 Thursday

READ
Mark 2

6:00

7:00

8:00

9:00

10:00

11:00

12:00

1:00

2:00

3:00

4:00

5:00

6:00

7:00

8:00

9:00

10:00

21 Friday

READ
Mark 3:1-19

6:00

7:00

8:00

9:00

10:00

11:00

12:00

1:00

2:00

3:00

4:00

5:00

6:00

7:00

8:00

9:00

10:00

22 Saturday

READ
Mark 3:20-35

6:00

7:00

8:00

9:00

10:00

11:00

12:00

1:00

2:00

3:00

4:00

5:00

6:00

7:00

8:00

9:00

10:00

What do you need to pray about this week?

To Do

Things you're thankful for this week:

23 Sunday

READ
Mark 4:1-20

6:00

7:00

8:00

9:00

10:00

11:00

12:00

1:00

2:00

3:00

4:00

5:00

6:00

7:00

8:00

9:00

10:00

24 Monday

READ
Mark 4:21-41

6:00

7:00

8:00

9:00

10:00

11:00

12:00

1:00

2:00

3:00

4:00

5:00

6:00

7:00

8:00

9:00

10:00

25 Tuesday

READ
Mark 5:1-20

6:00

7:00

8:00

9:00

10:00

11:00

12:00

1:00

2:00

3:00

4:00

5:00

6:00

7:00

8:00

9:00

10:00

26 Wednesday

READ
Mark 5:21-43

6:00

7:00

8:00

9:00

10:00

11:00

12:00

1:00

2:00

3:00

4:00

5:00

6:00

7:00

8:00

9:00

10:00

Jesus performed a lot of miracles during his ministry on earth. In every instance, he took advantage of the physical world around him and somehow changed it for good. What's one thing in your world you can change for good? Performing your own little "miracles" is a great way to stay Jesus-centered.

27 Thursday

READ
Mark 6:1-29

6:00

7:00

8:00

9:00

10:00

11:00

12:00

1:00

2:00

3:00

4:00

5:00

6:00

7:00

8:00

9:00

10:00

28 Friday

READ
Mark 6:30-44

6:00

7:00

8:00

9:00

10:00

11:00

12:00

1:00

2:00

3:00

4:00

5:00

6:00

7:00

8:00

9:00

10:00

29 Saturday

READ
Mark 6:45-56

6:00

7:00

8:00

9:00

10:00

11:00

12:00

1:00

2:00

3:00

4:00

5:00

6:00

7:00

8:00

9:00

10:00

What do you need to pray about this week?

To Do

Things you're thankful for this week:

Review your gratitude notes from the previous weeks, and write a prayer to Jesus thanking him for this month.

What experiences, insights, and moments kept you centered on Jesus this month? Record them here so you don't forget them.

Reviewing the previous month, how have you grown?

What is an area or two in which you'd like to continue to grow?

Review your appointments and tasks for the coming month. How are they aligned with Jesus' command to love others? Is there anything you need to cancel, add, or change? Pray about it; then update your schedule as needed.

Now write a prayer thanking Jesus for the month ahead, and include one way you're planning to stay focused on him.

MARCH 2020

To Do

Notes

Sunday	Monday	Tuesday
1	2	3
8	9	10
15	16	17
22	23	24
29	30	31

This month, focus on Jesus by...

Wednesday	Thursday	Friday	Saturday
4	5	6	7
11	12	13	14
18	19	20	21
25	26	27	28
1	2	3	4

Loving others: Who are you going to be intentional about showing love to this month? Write their names here, and schedule time to connect with them.

1 Sunday

READ
Mark 7:1-13

6:00

7:00

8:00

9:00

10:00

11:00

12:00

1:00

2:00

3:00

4:00

5:00

6:00

7:00

8:00

9:00

10:00

2 Monday

READ
Mark 7:14-37

6:00

7:00

8:00

9:00

10:00

11:00

12:00

1:00

2:00

3:00

4:00

5:00

6:00

7:00

8:00

9:00

10:00

3 Tuesday

READ
Mark 8

6:00

7:00

8:00

9:00

10:00

11:00

12:00

1:00

2:00

3:00

4:00

5:00

6:00

7:00

8:00

9:00

10:00

4 Wednesday

READ
Mark 9:1-29

6:00

7:00

8:00

9:00

10:00

11:00

12:00

1:00

2:00

3:00

4:00

5:00

6:00

7:00

8:00

9:00

10:00

It's hard to stay focused on Jesus when we have so many distractions all around us. Set aside some time this week to shut out the interference and concentrate on loving others—Jesus' main command for staying attached to him.

5 Thursday	6 Friday	7 Saturday	What do you need to pray about this week?
READ	READ	READ	
Mark 9:30-50	Mark 10:1-31	Mark 10:32-52	

5 Thursday

READ
Mark 9:30-50

6:00

7:00

8:00

9:00

10:00

11:00

12:00

1:00

2:00

3:00

4:00

5:00

6:00

7:00

8:00

9:00

10:00

6 Friday

READ
Mark 10:1-31

6:00

7:00

8:00

9:00

10:00

11:00

12:00

1:00

2:00

3:00

4:00

5:00

6:00

7:00

8:00

9:00

10:00

7 Saturday

READ
Mark 10:32-52

6:00

7:00

8:00

9:00

10:00

11:00

12:00

1:00

2:00

3:00

4:00

5:00

6:00

7:00

8:00

9:00

10:00

What do you need to pray about this week?

To Do

Things you're thankful for this week:

8 Sunday

READ
Mark 11:1-18

6:00

7:00

8:00

9:00

10:00

11:00

12:00

1:00

2:00

3:00

4:00

5:00

6:00

7:00

8:00

9:00

10:00

9 Monday

READ
Mark 11:19-33

6:00

7:00

8:00

9:00

10:00

11:00

12:00

1:00

2:00

3:00

4:00

5:00

6:00

7:00

8:00

9:00

10:00

10 Tuesday

READ
Mark 12:1-27

6:00

7:00

8:00

9:00

10:00

11:00

12:00

1:00

2:00

3:00

4:00

5:00

6:00

7:00

8:00

9:00

10:00

11 Wednesday

READ
Mark 12:28-44

6:00

7:00

8:00

9:00

10:00

11:00

12:00

1:00

2:00

3:00

4:00

5:00

6:00

7:00

8:00

9:00

10:00

In the planner's Bible reading for this week, a teacher asked Jesus which commandment was most important. Jesus said to love God and love others. The two go hand in hand; you can't do one without the other. How are you loving others this week?

12 Thursday

READE
Mark 13:1-20

6:00

7:00

8:00

9:00

10:00

11:00

12:00

1:00

2:00

3:00

4:00

5:00

6:00

7:00

8:00

9:00

10:00

13 Friday

READE
Mark 13:21-37

6:00

7:00

8:00

9:00

10:00

11:00

12:00

1:00

2:00

3:00

4:00

5:00

6:00

7:00

8:00

9:00

10:00

14 Saturday

READE
Mark 14:1-26

6:00

7:00

8:00

9:00

10:00

11:00

12:00

1:00

2:00

3:00

4:00

5:00

6:00

7:00

8:00

9:00

10:00

What do you need to pray about this week?

To Do

Things you're thankful for this week:

MAR 15 – MAR 21

15 Sunday
READ
Mark 14:27-53

6:00

7:00

8:00

9:00

10:00

11:00

12:00

1:00

2:00

3:00

4:00

5:00

6:00

7:00

8:00

9:00

10:00

16 Monday
READ
Mark 14:54-72

6:00

7:00

8:00

9:00

10:00

11:00

12:00

1:00

2:00

3:00

4:00

5:00

6:00

7:00

8:00

9:00

10:00

17 Tuesday
READ
Mark 15:1-25

6:00

7:00

8:00

9:00

10:00

11:00

12:00

1:00

2:00

3:00

4:00

5:00

6:00

7:00

8:00

9:00

10:00

18 Wednesday
READ
Mark 15:26-47

6:00

7:00

8:00

9:00

10:00

11:00

12:00

1:00

2:00

3:00

4:00

5:00

6:00

7:00

8:00

9:00

10:00

It can be helpful to keep daily routines when it comes to staying in Jesus' orbit. But sometimes we need to mix things up in order to be inspired and motivated anew. Try something creative in your focus on Jesus this week.

19 Thursday

READ
Mark 16

6:00

7:00

8:00

9:00

10:00

11:00

12:00

1:00

2:00

3:00

4:00

5:00

6:00

7:00

8:00

9:00

10:00

20 Friday

READ
Luke 1:1-20

6:00

7:00

8:00

9:00

10:00

11:00

12:00

1:00

2:00

3:00

4:00

5:00

6:00

7:00

8:00

9:00

10:00

21 Saturday

READ
Luke 1:21-38

6:00

7:00

8:00

9:00

10:00

11:00

12:00

1:00

2:00

3:00

4:00

5:00

6:00

7:00

8:00

9:00

10:00

What do you need to pray about this week?

To Do

Things you're thankful for this week:

MAR 22 – MAR 28

22 Sunday	23 Monday	24 Tuesday	25 Wednesday
READ	READ	READ	READ
Luke 1:39-56	*Luke 1:57-80*	*Luke 2:1-24*	*Luke 2:25-52*

6:00	6:00	6:00	6:00
7:00	7:00	7:00	7:00
8:00	8:00	8:00	8:00
9:00	9:00	9:00	9:00
10:00	10:00	10:00	10:00
11:00	11:00	11:00	11:00
12:00	12:00	12:00	12:00
1:00	1:00	1:00	1:00
2:00	2:00	2:00	2:00
3:00	3:00	3:00	3:00
4:00	4:00	4:00	4:00
5:00	5:00	5:00	5:00
6:00	6:00	6:00	6:00
7:00	7:00	7:00	7:00
8:00	8:00	8:00	8:00
9:00	9:00	9:00	9:00
10:00	10:00	10:00	10:00

If you're not actively and regularly loving others, you're not truly centered on Jesus. Make it your number-one priority to show love to at least three people this week. Even small things can make a big difference.

26 Thursday

READ
Luke 3

6:00

7:00

8:00

9:00

10:00

11:00

12:00

1:00

2:00

3:00

4:00

5:00

6:00

7:00

8:00

9:00

10:00

27 Friday

READ
Luke 4:1-30

6:00

7:00

8:00

9:00

10:00

11:00

12:00

1:00

2:00

3:00

4:00

5:00

6:00

7:00

8:00

9:00

10:00

28 Saturday

READ
Luke 4:31-44

6:00

7:00

8:00

9:00

10:00

11:00

12:00

1:00

2:00

3:00

4:00

5:00

6:00

7:00

8:00

9:00

10:00

What do you need to pray about this week?

To Do

Things you're thankful for this week:

Review your gratitude notes from the previous weeks, and write a prayer to Jesus thanking him for this month.

What experiences, insights, and moments kept you centered on Jesus this month? Record them here so you don't forget them.

Reviewing the previous month, how have you grown?

What is an area or two in which you'd like to continue to grow?

Review your appointments and tasks for the coming month. How are they aligned with Jesus' command to love others? Is there anything you need to cancel, add, or change? Pray about it; then update your schedule as needed.

Now write a prayer thanking Jesus for the month ahead, and include one way you're planning to stay focused on him.

Setting Jesus-Centered Goals, Second Quarter

Look to Jesus' example to guide you during your goal-setting.

Before committing to goals, spend 5 to 10 minutes writing or mapping a sketch of everything that's currently on your heart relating to your dreams and aspirations. Don't edit yourself; it's okay if this list includes your most personal desires or things that seem impossible. Be open and honest with yourself about where your heart is right now.

Now think about Jesus' command to love others. How are Jesus' words connected to your own dreams and aspirations? Pray about it. Challenge yourself to be open to what that really means for you. If staying attached to Jesus is all about loving others, how will that affect your goals? If needed, rework your goals here.

With Jesus' command in mind, prayerfully consider one to three goals you can set for yourself for this quarter.

QUARTERLY GOAL (APRIL, MAY, JUNE)

Achieving this goal is important to you because…

Achieving this goal is important to Jesus because…

ACTION STEPS needed to accomplish this goal…

If you've identified one or two other quarterly goals, write them here along with the reasons they're important and the action steps you'll take to achieve them.

To Do

Notes

Sunday	Monday	Tuesday
29	30	31
5	6	7
12	13	14
Easter Sunday		
19	20	21
26	27	28

This month, focus on Jesus by...

Wednesday	Thursday	Friday	Saturday
1	2	3	4
8	9	10 Good Friday	11
15	16	17	18
22	23	24	25
29	30	1	2

Loving others: Who are you going to be intentional about showing love to this month? Write their names here, and schedule time to connect with them.

29 Sunday
READ
Luke 5:1-16

6:00	
7:00	
8:00	
9:00	
10:00	
11:00	
12:00	
1:00	
2:00	
3:00	
4:00	
5:00	
6:00	
7:00	
8:00	
9:00	
10:00	

30 Monday
READ
Luke 5:17-39

6:00	
7:00	
8:00	
9:00	
10:00	
11:00	
12:00	
1:00	
2:00	
3:00	
4:00	
5:00	
6:00	
7:00	
8:00	
9:00	
10:00	

31 Tuesday
READ
Luke 6:1-26

6:00	
7:00	
8:00	
9:00	
10:00	
11:00	
12:00	
1:00	
2:00	
3:00	
4:00	
5:00	
6:00	
7:00	
8:00	
9:00	
10:00	

1 Wednesday
READ
Luke 6:27-49

6:00	
7:00	
8:00	
9:00	
10:00	
11:00	
12:00	
1:00	
2:00	
3:00	
4:00	
5:00	
6:00	
7:00	
8:00	
9:00	
10:00	

Centering your life on Jesus involves understanding and accepting Jesus' views on the true nature of love, which includes loving your enemies. Who's someone in your immediate life you find hard to love? What's one thing you can do to show love to that person? (Reading 1 Corinthians 13:4-7 may help.)

2 Thursday

READ
Luke 7:1-30

6:00

7:00

8:00

9:00

10:00

11:00

12:00

1:00

2:00

3:00

4:00

5:00

6:00

7:00

8:00

9:00

10:00

3 Friday

READ
Luke 7:31-50

6:00

7:00

8:00

9:00

10:00

11:00

12:00

1:00

2:00

3:00

4:00

5:00

6:00

7:00

8:00

9:00

10:00

4 Saturday

READ
Luke 8:1-25

6:00

7:00

8:00

9:00

10:00

11:00

12:00

1:00

2:00

3:00

4:00

5:00

6:00

7:00

8:00

9:00

10:00

What do you need to pray about this week?

To Do

Things you're thankful for this week:

5 Sunday

READ
Luke 8:26-56

6:00

7:00

8:00

9:00

10:00

11:00

12:00

1:00

2:00

3:00

4:00

5:00

6:00

7:00

8:00

9:00

10:00

6 Monday

READ
Luke 9:1-17

6:00

7:00

8:00

9:00

10:00

11:00

12:00

1:00

2:00

3:00

4:00

5:00

6:00

7:00

8:00

9:00

10:00

7 Tuesday

READ
Luke 9:18-36

6:00

7:00

8:00

9:00

10:00

11:00

12:00

1:00

2:00

3:00

4:00

5:00

6:00

7:00

8:00

9:00

10:00

8 Wednesday

READ
Luke 9:37-62

6:00

7:00

8:00

9:00

10:00

11:00

12:00

1:00

2:00

3:00

4:00

5:00

6:00

7:00

8:00

9:00

10:00

It's one thing to minimize distractions in your life. It's quite another to eliminate them completely, especially when it comes to centering your life on Jesus. What's one thing that's holding you back from a deeper devotion to Jesus?

9 Thursday

READ
Luke 10:1-24

6:00

7:00

8:00

9:00

10:00

11:00

12:00

1:00

2:00

3:00

4:00

5:00

6:00

7:00

8:00

9:00

10:00

10 Friday

READ
Luke 10:25-42

6:00

7:00

8:00

9:00

10:00

11:00

12:00

1:00

2:00

3:00

4:00

5:00

6:00

7:00

8:00

9:00

10:00

11 Saturday

READ
Luke 11:1-28

6:00

7:00

8:00

9:00

10:00

11:00

12:00

1:00

2:00

3:00

4:00

5:00

6:00

7:00

8:00

9:00

10:00

What do you need to pray about this week?

To Do

Things you're thankful for this week:

12 Sunday

READ
Luke 11:29-54

6:00

7:00

8:00

9:00

10:00

11:00

12:00

1:00

2:00

3:00

4:00

5:00

6:00

7:00

8:00

9:00

10:00

13 Monday

READ
Luke 12:1-31

6:00

7:00

8:00

9:00

10:00

11:00

12:00

1:00

2:00

3:00

4:00

5:00

6:00

7:00

8:00

9:00

10:00

14 Tuesday

READ
Luke 12:32-59

6:00

7:00

8:00

9:00

10:00

11:00

12:00

1:00

2:00

3:00

4:00

5:00

6:00

7:00

8:00

9:00

10:00

15 Wednesday

READ
Luke 13:1-22

6:00

7:00

8:00

9:00

10:00

11:00

12:00

1:00

2:00

3:00

4:00

5:00

6:00

7:00

8:00

9:00

10:00

Perhaps instead of eliminating a distraction from your life, you can find a way to use that experience to help you focus more on Jesus. Find a nonspiritual-related activity on your schedule this week. How can you bring Jesus into that moment?

16 Thursday

READ
Luke 13:23-35

6:00

7:00

8:00

9:00

10:00

11:00

12:00

1:00

2:00

3:00

4:00

5:00

6:00

7:00

8:00

9:00

10:00

17 Friday

READ
Luke 14:1-24

6:00

7:00

8:00

9:00

10:00

11:00

12:00

1:00

2:00

3:00

4:00

5:00

6:00

7:00

8:00

9:00

10:00

18 Saturday

READ
Luke 14:25-35

6:00

7:00

8:00

9:00

10:00

11:00

12:00

1:00

2:00

3:00

4:00

5:00

6:00

7:00

8:00

9:00

10:00

What do you need to pray about this week?

To Do

Things you're thankful for this week:

APR 19 – APR 25

19 Sunday

READ
Luke 15:1-10

6:00

7:00

8:00

9:00

10:00

11:00

12:00

1:00

2:00

3:00

4:00

5:00

6:00

7:00

8:00

9:00

10:00

20 Monday

READ
Luke 15:11-32

6:00

7:00

8:00

9:00

10:00

11:00

12:00

1:00

2:00

3:00

4:00

5:00

6:00

7:00

8:00

9:00

10:00

21 Tuesday

READ
Luke 16

6:00

7:00

8:00

9:00

10:00

11:00

12:00

1:00

2:00

3:00

4:00

5:00

6:00

7:00

8:00

9:00

10:00

22 Wednesday

READ
Luke 17:1-19

6:00

7:00

8:00

9:00

10:00

11:00

12:00

1:00

2:00

3:00

4:00

5:00

6:00

7:00

8:00

9:00

10:00

We all have to-do lists. But do you have a "to-be" list? Who does Jesus want you to become as you pursue a closer relationship with him? Think of one characteristic, and schedule some time to meditate on and pray about it this week.

23 Thursday

READimage
Luke 17:20-37

6:00

7:00

8:00

9:00

10:00

11:00

12:00

1:00

2:00

3:00

4:00

5:00

6:00

7:00

8:00

9:00

10:00

24 Friday

READ
Luke 18:1-23

6:00

7:00

8:00

9:00

10:00

11:00

12:00

1:00

2:00

3:00

4:00

5:00

6:00

7:00

8:00

9:00

10:00

25 Saturday

READ
Luke 18:24-43

6:00

7:00

8:00

9:00

10:00

11:00

12:00

1:00

2:00

3:00

4:00

5:00

6:00

7:00

8:00

9:00

10:00

What do you need to pray about this week?

To Do

Things you're thankful for this week:

26 Sunday

READ
Luke 19:1-27

6:00

7:00

8:00

9:00

10:00

11:00

12:00

1:00

2:00

3:00

4:00

5:00

6:00

7:00

8:00

9:00

10:00

27 Monday

READ
Luke 19:28-48

6:00

7:00

8:00

9:00

10:00

11:00

12:00

1:00

2:00

3:00

4:00

5:00

6:00

7:00

8:00

9:00

10:00

28 Tuesday

READ
Luke 20:1-26

6:00

7:00

8:00

9:00

10:00

11:00

12:00

1:00

2:00

3:00

4:00

5:00

6:00

7:00

8:00

9:00

10:00

29 Wednesday

READ
Luke 20:27-47

6:00

7:00

8:00

9:00

10:00

11:00

12:00

1:00

2:00

3:00

4:00

5:00

6:00

7:00

8:00

9:00

10:00

Jesus cares about relationships more than anything else. Take a look at all your appointments you have scheduled for this week. How many are focused on nourishing a relationship, either with Jesus or another person? Which one(s) could be? Is there a relational appointment you need to add?

30 Thursday	1 Friday	2 Saturday	What do you need to pray about this week?
READ	READ	READ	
Luke 21:1-19	*Luke 21:20-38*	*Luke 22:1-30*	
6:00	6:00	6:00	
7:00	7:00	7:00	
8:00	8:00	8:00	
9:00	9:00	9:00	
10:00	10:00	10:00	
11:00	11:00	11:00	
12:00	12:00	12:00	
1:00	1:00	1:00	
2:00	2:00	2:00	
3:00	3:00	3:00	*To Do*
4:00	4:00	4:00	
5:00	5:00	5:00	
6:00	6:00	6:00	
7:00	7:00	7:00	
8:00	8:00	8:00	
9:00	9:00	9:00	
10:00	10:00	10:00	

Things you're thankful for this week:

Review your gratitude notes from the previous weeks, and write a prayer to Jesus thanking him for this month.

What experiences, insights, and moments kept you centered on Jesus this month? Record them here so you don't forget them.

Reviewing the previous month, how have you grown?

What is an area or two in which you'd like to continue to grow?

Review your appointments and tasks for the coming month. How are they aligned with Jesus' command to love others? Is there anything you need to cancel, add, or change? Pray about it; then update your schedule as needed.

Now write a prayer thanking Jesus for the month ahead, and include one way you're planning to stay focused on him.

To Do

Notes

Sunday	Monday	Tuesday
26	27	28
3	4	5
10	11	12
17 Mother's Day	18	19
24	25 Memorial Day	26
31	1	2

This month, focus on Jesus by...

Wednesday	Thursday	Friday	Saturday
29	30	1	2
6	7	8	9
13	14	15	16
20	21	22	23
27	28	29	30
3	4	5	6

Loving others: Who are you going to be intentional about showing love to this month? Write their names here, and schedule time to connect with them.

3 Sunday

READR
Luke 22:31-46

6:00

7:00

8:00

9:00

10:00

11:00

12:00

1:00

2:00

3:00

4:00

5:00

6:00

7:00

8:00

9:00

10:00

4 Monday

READ
Luke 22:47-71

6:00

7:00

8:00

9:00

10:00

11:00

12:00

1:00

2:00

3:00

4:00

5:00

6:00

7:00

8:00

9:00

10:00

5 Tuesday

READ
Luke 23:1-25

6:00

7:00

8:00

9:00

10:00

11:00

12:00

1:00

2:00

3:00

4:00

5:00

6:00

7:00

8:00

9:00

10:00

6 Wednesday

READ
Luke 23:26-56

6:00

7:00

8:00

9:00

10:00

11:00

12:00

1:00

2:00

3:00

4:00

5:00

6:00

7:00

8:00

9:00

10:00

Many, if not most, of the most important moments of your week aren't on your schedule. Spontaneous experiences are likely to flow out of the priorities in your life. How many unplanned moments with Jesus have you been having lately?

7 Thursday

READM
Luke 24:1-35

6:00

7:00

8:00

9:00

10:00

11:00

12:00

1:00

2:00

3:00

4:00

5:00

6:00

7:00

8:00

9:00

10:00

8 Friday

READM
Luke 24:36-53

6:00

7:00

8:00

9:00

10:00

11:00

12:00

1:00

2:00

3:00

4:00

5:00

6:00

7:00

8:00

9:00

10:00

9 Saturday

READM
John 1:1-28

6:00

7:00

8:00

9:00

10:00

11:00

12:00

1:00

2:00

3:00

4:00

5:00

6:00

7:00

8:00

9:00

10:00

What do you need to pray about this week?

To Do

Things you're thankful for this week:

10 Sunday

READ
John 1:29-51

6:00

7:00

8:00

9:00

10:00

11:00

12:00

1:00

2:00

3:00

4:00

5:00

6:00

7:00

8:00

9:00

10:00

11 Monday

READ
John 2

6:00

7:00

8:00

9:00

10:00

11:00

12:00

1:00

2:00

3:00

4:00

5:00

6:00

7:00

8:00

9:00

10:00

12 Tuesday

READ
John 3:1-18

6:00

7:00

8:00

9:00

10:00

11:00

12:00

1:00

2:00

3:00

4:00

5:00

6:00

7:00

8:00

9:00

10:00

13 Wednesday

READ
John 3:19-36

6:00

7:00

8:00

9:00

10:00

11:00

12:00

1:00

2:00

3:00

4:00

5:00

6:00

7:00

8:00

9:00

10:00

*Being centered on Jesus doesn't necessarily mean always **feeling** close to Jesus. True love takes action whether or not we feel like it. Maybe this is a week you don't feel like going out of your way to show love to someone— which may be all the more reason to do it.*

14 Thursday

READ
John 4:1-30

6:00

7:00

8:00

9:00

10:00

11:00

12:00

1:00

2:00

3:00

4:00

5:00

6:00

7:00

8:00

9:00

10:00

15 Friday

READ
John 4:31-54

6:00

7:00

8:00

9:00

10:00

11:00

12:00

1:00

2:00

3:00

4:00

5:00

6:00

7:00

8:00

9:00

10:00

16 Saturday

READ
John 5:1-24

6:00

7:00

8:00

9:00

10:00

11:00

12:00

1:00

2:00

3:00

4:00

5:00

6:00

7:00

8:00

9:00

10:00

What do you need to pray about this week?

To Do

Things you're thankful for this week:

17 Sunday

READ
John 5:25-47

6:00

7:00

8:00

9:00

10:00

11:00

12:00

1:00

2:00

3:00

4:00

5:00

6:00

7:00

8:00

9:00

10:00

18 Monday

READ
John 6:1-21

6:00

7:00

8:00

9:00

10:00

11:00

12:00

1:00

2:00

3:00

4:00

5:00

6:00

7:00

8:00

9:00

10:00

19 Tuesday

READ
John 6:22-44

6:00

7:00

8:00

9:00

10:00

11:00

12:00

1:00

2:00

3:00

4:00

5:00

6:00

7:00

8:00

9:00

10:00

20 Wednesday

READ
John 6:45-71

6:00

7:00

8:00

9:00

10:00

11:00

12:00

1:00

2:00

3:00

4:00

5:00

6:00

7:00

8:00

9:00

10:00

Feeling busy this week? Sometimes our calendars can be so full that our week can feel like a blur. Those may be the times Jesus looks a little blurry to you, too. But you can always find a moment—no matter how small—to stop, take a breath, and give Jesus your complete attention, to find your true center again.

21 Thursday
READ
John 7:1-27

6:00

7:00

8:00

9:00

10:00

11:00

12:00

1:00

2:00

3:00

4:00

5:00

6:00

7:00

8:00

9:00

10:00

22 Friday
READ
John 7:28-53

6:00

7:00

8:00

9:00

10:00

11:00

12:00

1:00

2:00

3:00

4:00

5:00

6:00

7:00

8:00

9:00

10:00

23 Saturday
READ
John 8:1-27

6:00

7:00

8:00

9:00

10:00

11:00

12:00

1:00

2:00

3:00

4:00

5:00

6:00

7:00

8:00

9:00

10:00

What do you need to pray about this week?

To Do

Things you're thankful for this week:

24 Sunday
READ
John 8:28-59

6:00

7:00

8:00

9:00

10:00

11:00

12:00

1:00

2:00

3:00

4:00

5:00

6:00

7:00

8:00

9:00

10:00

25 Monday
READ
John 9:1-23

6:00

7:00

8:00

9:00

10:00

11:00

12:00

1:00

2:00

3:00

4:00

5:00

6:00

7:00

8:00

9:00

10:00

26 Tuesday
READ
John 9:24-41

6:00

7:00

8:00

9:00

10:00

11:00

12:00

1:00

2:00

3:00

4:00

5:00

6:00

7:00

8:00

9:00

10:00

27 Wednesday
READ
John 10:1-23

6:00

7:00

8:00

9:00

10:00

11:00

12:00

1:00

2:00

3:00

4:00

5:00

6:00

7:00

8:00

9:00

10:00

The best cure for unhappiness is to stop focusing on yourself. Self-care is important, but so is loving others. Remember, that's the real key to being centered on Jesus. If you find yourself downhearted this week, find a way to lift someone else's spirits. It's guaranteed to lift yours as well.

28 Thursday

READS
John 10:24-42

6:00

7:00

8:00

9:00

10:00

11:00

12:00

1:00

2:00

3:00

4:00

5:00

6:00

7:00

8:00

9:00

10:00

29 Friday

READS
John 11:1-29

6:00

7:00

8:00

9:00

10:00

11:00

12:00

1:00

2:00

3:00

4:00

5:00

6:00

7:00

8:00

9:00

10:00

30 Saturday

READS
John 11:30-57

6:00

7:00

8:00

9:00

10:00

11:00

12:00

1:00

2:00

3:00

4:00

5:00

6:00

7:00

8:00

9:00

10:00

What do you need to pray about this week?

To Do

Things you're thankful for this week:

Review your gratitude notes from the previous weeks, and write a prayer to Jesus thanking him for this month.

_____
_____
_____
_____
_____
_____
_____
_____
_____
_____
_____
_____
_____
_____
_____
_____

What experiences, insights, and moments kept you centered on Jesus this month? Record them here so you don't forget them.

_____
_____
_____
_____
_____
_____
_____
_____
_____
_____
_____
_____
_____
_____
_____
_____

Reviewing the previous month, how have you grown?

What is an area or two in which you'd like to continue to grow?

Review your appointments and tasks for the coming month. How are they aligned with Jesus' command to love others? Is there anything you need to cancel, add, or change? Pray about it; then update your schedule as needed.

Now write a prayer thanking Jesus for the month ahead, and include one way you're planning to stay focused on him.

JUNE 2020

	Sunday	Monday	Tuesday
	31	1	2
	7	8	9
	14	15	16
	21	22	23
	Father's Day 28	29	30

Notes

This month, focus on Jesus by...

Wednesday	Thursday	Friday	Saturday
3	4	5	6
10	11	12	13
17	18	19	20
24	25	26	27
1	2	3	4

Loving others: Who are you going to be intentional about showing love to this month? Write their names here, and schedule time to connect with them.

MAY 31 – JUNE 6

31 Sunday	*1 Monday*	*2 Tuesday*	*3 Wednesday*
READ *John 12:1-26*	READ *John 12:27-50*	READ *John 13:1-20*	READ *John 13:21-38*
6:00	6:00	6:00	6:00
7:00	7:00	7:00	7:00
8:00	8:00	8:00	8:00
9:00	9:00	9:00	9:00
10:00	10:00	10:00	10:00
11:00	11:00	11:00	11:00
12:00	12:00	12:00	12:00
1:00	1:00	1:00	1:00
2:00	2:00	2:00	2:00
3:00	3:00	3:00	3:00
4:00	4:00	4:00	4:00
5:00	5:00	5:00	5:00
6:00	6:00	6:00	6:00
7:00	7:00	7:00	7:00
8:00	8:00	8:00	8:00
9:00	9:00	9:00	9:00
10:00	10:00	10:00	10:00

On a scale of 1 to 10, how peaceful do you feel right now? To be Jesus-centered is to be at peace, if Colossians 3:15 and Galatians 5:22 are to be believed. And if you're struggling to find peace, consider being a peacemaker. (See Hebrews 12:14 and Matthew 5:9.)

4 Thursday

READ
John 14

6:00

7:00

8:00

9:00

10:00

11:00

12:00

1:00

2:00

3:00

4:00

5:00

6:00

7:00

8:00

9:00

10:00

5 Friday

READ
John 15

6:00

7:00

8:00

9:00

10:00

11:00

12:00

1:00

2:00

3:00

4:00

5:00

6:00

7:00

8:00

9:00

10:00

6 Saturday

READ
John 16

6:00

7:00

8:00

9:00

10:00

11:00

12:00

1:00

2:00

3:00

4:00

5:00

6:00

7:00

8:00

9:00

10:00

What do you need to pray about this week?

To Do

Things you're thankful for this week:

JUNE 7 – JUNE 13

7 Sunday	8 Monday	9 Tuesday	10 Wednesday
READ	READ	READ	READ
John 17	*John 18:1-18*	*John 18:19-40*	*John 19:1-22*
6:00	6:00	6:00	6:00
7:00	7:00	7:00	7:00
8:00	8:00	8:00	8:00
9:00	9:00	9:00	9:00
10:00	10:00	10:00	10:00
11:00	11:00	11:00	11:00
12:00	12:00	12:00	12:00
1:00	1:00	1:00	1:00
2:00	2:00	2:00	2:00
3:00	3:00	3:00	3:00
4:00	4:00	4:00	4:00
5:00	5:00	5:00	5:00
6:00	6:00	6:00	6:00
7:00	7:00	7:00	7:00
8:00	8:00	8:00	8:00
9:00	9:00	9:00	9:00
10:00	10:00	10:00	10:00

Does joy seem to come to you naturally? Or do you find yourself having to go hunt for it? Jesus wants joy in your life. Schedule an activity this week that brings you joy. Be sure to invite Jesus along!

11 Thursday

READ
John 19:23-42

6:00

7:00

8:00

9:00

10:00

11:00

12:00

1:00

2:00

3:00

4:00

5:00

6:00

7:00

8:00

9:00

10:00

12 Friday

READ
John 20

6:00

7:00

8:00

9:00

10:00

11:00

12:00

1:00

2:00

3:00

4:00

5:00

6:00

7:00

8:00

9:00

10:00

13 Saturday

READ
John 21

6:00

7:00

8:00

9:00

10:00

11:00

12:00

1:00

2:00

3:00

4:00

5:00

6:00

7:00

8:00

9:00

10:00

What do you need to pray about this week?

To Do

Things you're thankful for this week:

14 Sunday
READ
Acts 1

6:00

7:00

8:00

9:00

10:00

11:00

12:00

1:00

2:00

3:00

4:00

5:00

6:00

7:00

8:00

9:00

10:00

15 Monday
READ
Acts 2:1-21

6:00

7:00

8:00

9:00

10:00

11:00

12:00

1:00

2:00

3:00

4:00

5:00

6:00

7:00

8:00

9:00

10:00

16 Tuesday
READ
Acts 2:22-47

6:00

7:00

8:00

9:00

10:00

11:00

12:00

1:00

2:00

3:00

4:00

5:00

6:00

7:00

8:00

9:00

10:00

17 Wednesday
READ
Acts 3

6:00

7:00

8:00

9:00

10:00

11:00

12:00

1:00

2:00

3:00

4:00

5:00

6:00

7:00

8:00

9:00

10:00

One of the greatest gifts you can give another person is grace. To offer mercy and goodwill in difficult circumstances is a pure act of love. Is there someone you know who's struggling right now? Be Jesus-centered this week and bring some grace into his or her life.

18 Thursday

READ
Acts 4:1-22

6:00

7:00

8:00

9:00

10:00

11:00

12:00

1:00

2:00

3:00

4:00

5:00

6:00

7:00

8:00

9:00

10:00

19 Friday

READ
Acts 4:23-37

6:00

7:00

8:00

9:00

10:00

11:00

12:00

1:00

2:00

3:00

4:00

5:00

6:00

7:00

8:00

9:00

10:00

20 Saturday

READ
Acts 5:1-21

6:00

7:00

8:00

9:00

10:00

11:00

12:00

1:00

2:00

3:00

4:00

5:00

6:00

7:00

8:00

9:00

10:00

What do you need to pray about this week?

To Do

Things you're thankful for this week:

21 Sunday
READ
Acts 5:22-42

6:00

7:00

8:00

9:00

10:00

11:00

12:00

1:00

2:00

3:00

4:00

5:00

6:00

7:00

8:00

9:00

10:00

22 Monday
READ
Acts 6

6:00

7:00

8:00

9:00

10:00

11:00

12:00

1:00

2:00

3:00

4:00

5:00

6:00

7:00

8:00

9:00

10:00

23 Tuesday
READ
Acts 7:1-21

6:00

7:00

8:00

9:00

10:00

11:00

12:00

1:00

2:00

3:00

4:00

5:00

6:00

7:00

8:00

9:00

10:00

24 Wednesday
READ
Acts 7:22-43

6:00

7:00

8:00

9:00

10:00

11:00

12:00

1:00

2:00

3:00

4:00

5:00

6:00

7:00

8:00

9:00

10:00

You're halfway through the year! How are you doing with your 2020 vision and keeping your focus on Jesus? If you've made it this far into your planner, then you've definitely moved closer to Jesus (whether you think it or feel like it). Keep moving forward!

25 Thursday

READ
Acts 7:44-60

6:00

7:00

8:00

9:00

10:00

11:00

12:00

1:00

2:00

3:00

4:00

5:00

6:00

7:00

8:00

9:00

10:00

26 Friday

READ
Acts 8:1-25

6:00

7:00

8:00

9:00

10:00

11:00

12:00

1:00

2:00

3:00

4:00

5:00

6:00

7:00

8:00

9:00

10:00

27 Saturday

READ
Acts 8:26-40

6:00

7:00

8:00

9:00

10:00

11:00

12:00

1:00

2:00

3:00

4:00

5:00

6:00

7:00

8:00

9:00

10:00

What do you need to pray about this week?

To Do

Things you're thankful for this week:

Review your gratitude notes from the previous weeks, and write a prayer to Jesus thanking him for this month.

What experiences, insights, and moments kept you centered on Jesus this month? Record them here so you don't forget them.

Reviewing the previous month, how have you grown?

What is an area or two in which you'd like to continue to grow?

Review your appointments and tasks for the coming month. How are they aligned with Jesus' command to love others? Is there anything you need to cancel, add, or change? Pray about it; then update your schedule as needed.

Now write a prayer thanking Jesus for the month ahead, and include one way you're planning to stay focused on him.

Setting Jesus-Centered Goals, Third Quarter

Look to Jesus' example to guide you during your goal-setting.

Before committing to goals, spend 5 to 10 minutes writing or mapping a sketch of everything that's currently on your heart relating to your dreams and aspirations. Don't edit yourself; it's okay if this list includes your most personal desires or things that seem impossible. Be open and honest with yourself about where your heart is right now.

Now think about Jesus' command to love others. How are Jesus' words connected to your own dreams and aspirations? Pray about it. Challenge yourself to be open to what that really means for you. If staying attached to Jesus is all about loving others, how will that affect your goals? If needed, rework your goals here.

With Jesus' command in mind, prayerfully consider one to three goals you can set for yourself for this quarter.

QUARTERLY GOAL (JULY, AUGUST, SEPTEMBER)

Achieving this goal is important to you because…

Achieving this goal is important to Jesus because…

ACTION STEPS needed to accomplish this goal…

If you've identified one or two other quarterly goals, write them here along with the reasons they're important and the action steps you'll take to achieve them.

To Do

Notes

Sunday	Monday	Tuesday
28	29	30
5	6	7
12	13	14
19	20	21
26	27	28

This month, focus on Jesus by...

Wednesday	Thursday	Friday	Saturday
1	2	3	4 Independence Day
8	9	10	11
15	16	17	18
22	23	24	25
29	30	31	1

Loving others: Who are you going to be intentional about showing love to this month? Write their names here, and schedule time to connect with them.

JUNE 28 – JULY 4

28 Sunday	*29 Monday*	*30 Tuesday*	*1 Wednesday*
READ	READ	READ	READ
Acts 9:1-21	*Acts 9:22-43*	*Acts 10:1-23*	*Acts 10:24-48*
6:00	6:00	6:00	6:00
7:00	7:00	7:00	7:00
8:00	8:00	8:00	8:00
9:00	9:00	9:00	9:00
10:00	10:00	10:00	10:00
11:00	11:00	11:00	11:00
12:00	12:00	12:00	12:00
1:00	1:00	1:00	1:00
2:00	2:00	2:00	2:00
3:00	3:00	3:00	3:00
4:00	4:00	4:00	4:00
5:00	5:00	5:00	5:00
6:00	6:00	6:00	6:00
7:00	7:00	7:00	7:00
8:00	8:00	8:00	8:00
9:00	9:00	9:00	9:00
10:00	10:00	10:00	10:00

Jesus doesn't belong in a box. To be Jesus-centered doesn't mean putting Jesus in a spot and leaving him there while you get along with the rest of your life. Putting Jesus at the center means your entire life orbits around him. Don't compartmentalize Jesus; welcome him into every part of your life.

2 Thursday

READ
Acts 11

6:00

7:00

8:00

9:00

10:00

11:00

12:00

1:00

2:00

3:00

4:00

5:00

6:00

7:00

8:00

9:00

10:00

3 Friday

READ
Acts 12

6:00

7:00

8:00

9:00

10:00

11:00

12:00

1:00

2:00

3:00

4:00

5:00

6:00

7:00

8:00

9:00

10:00

4 Saturday

READ
Acts 13:1-25

6:00

7:00

8:00

9:00

10:00

11:00

12:00

1:00

2:00

3:00

4:00

5:00

6:00

7:00

8:00

9:00

10:00

What do you need to pray about this week?

To Do

Things you're thankful for this week:

5 Sunday

READ
Acts 13:26-52

6:00	
7:00	
8:00	
9:00	
10:00	
11:00	
12:00	
1:00	
2:00	
3:00	
4:00	
5:00	
6:00	
7:00	
8:00	
9:00	
10:00	

6 Monday

READ
Acts 14

6:00	
7:00	
8:00	
9:00	
10:00	
11:00	
12:00	
1:00	
2:00	
3:00	
4:00	
5:00	
6:00	
7:00	
8:00	
9:00	
10:00	

7 Tuesday

READ
Acts 15:1-21

6:00	
7:00	
8:00	
9:00	
10:00	
11:00	
12:00	
1:00	
2:00	
3:00	
4:00	
5:00	
6:00	
7:00	
8:00	
9:00	
10:00	

8 Wednesday

READ
Acts 15:22-41

6:00	
7:00	
8:00	
9:00	
10:00	
11:00	
12:00	
1:00	
2:00	
3:00	
4:00	
5:00	
6:00	
7:00	
8:00	
9:00	
10:00	

Today's society has a highly divisive political climate. It's all too easy to let disagreements turn people into enemies. But Jesus said to love your enemies. Make some time this week—even schedule it if you can—to reach out to someone on the "other side" and show that person genuine kindness.

9 Thursday
READ
Acts 16:1-21

6:00

7:00

8:00

9:00

10:00

11:00

12:00

1:00

2:00

3:00

4:00

5:00

6:00

7:00

8:00

9:00

10:00

10 Friday
READ
Acts 16:22-40

6:00

7:00

8:00

9:00

10:00

11:00

12:00

1:00

2:00

3:00

4:00

5:00

6:00

7:00

8:00

9:00

10:00

11 Saturday
READ
Acts 17:1-15

6:00

7:00

8:00

9:00

10:00

11:00

12:00

1:00

2:00

3:00

4:00

5:00

6:00

7:00

8:00

9:00

10:00

What do you need to pray about this week?

To Do

Things you're thankful for this week:

12 Sunday
READ
Acts 17:16-34

6:00

7:00

8:00

9:00

10:00

11:00

12:00

1:00

2:00

3:00

4:00

5:00

6:00

7:00

8:00

9:00

10:00

13 Monday
READ
Acts 18

6:00

7:00

8:00

9:00

10:00

11:00

12:00

1:00

2:00

3:00

4:00

5:00

6:00

7:00

8:00

9:00

10:00

14 Tuesday
READ
Acts 19:1-20

6:00

7:00

8:00

9:00

10:00

11:00

12:00

1:00

2:00

3:00

4:00

5:00

6:00

7:00

8:00

9:00

10:00

15 Wednesday
READ
Acts 19:21-41

6:00

7:00

8:00

9:00

10:00

11:00

12:00

1:00

2:00

3:00

4:00

5:00

6:00

7:00

8:00

9:00

10:00

*After penciling in your appointments for the week, step back and think about **why** your week is scheduled the way it is. Would you say your week ahead is Jesus-centered? Why or why not? What's one thing you can do to make Jesus the focus of your time?*

16 Thursday

READ
Acts 20:1-16

6:00

7:00

8:00

9:00

10:00

11:00

12:00

1:00

2:00

3:00

4:00

5:00

6:00

7:00

8:00

9:00

10:00

17 Friday

READ
Acts 20:17-38

6:00

7:00

8:00

9:00

10:00

11:00

12:00

1:00

2:00

3:00

4:00

5:00

6:00

7:00

8:00

9:00

10:00

18 Saturday

READ
Acts 21:1-17

6:00

7:00

8:00

9:00

10:00

11:00

12:00

1:00

2:00

3:00

4:00

5:00

6:00

7:00

8:00

9:00

10:00

What do you need to pray about this week?

To Do

Things you're thankful for this week:

19 Sunday	20 Monday	21 Tuesday	22 Wednesday
READ	READ	READ	READ
Acts 21:18-40	*Acts 22*	*Acts 23:1-15*	*Acts 23:16-35*
6:00	6:00	6:00	6:00
7:00	7:00	7:00	7:00
8:00	8:00	8:00	8:00
9:00	9:00	9:00	9:00
10:00	10:00	10:00	10:00
11:00	11:00	11:00	11:00
12:00	12:00	12:00	12:00
1:00	1:00	1:00	1:00
2:00	2:00	2:00	2:00
3:00	3:00	3:00	3:00
4:00	4:00	4:00	4:00
5:00	5:00	5:00	5:00
6:00	6:00	6:00	6:00
7:00	7:00	7:00	7:00
8:00	8:00	8:00	8:00
9:00	9:00	9:00	9:00
10:00	10:00	10:00	10:00

*What do you think Jesus would have to say about your schedule this week? Jesus did have some things to say about what we ought to focus on. He said don't focus on things like money, food, and clothes. Instead, Jesus tells us to spend our time on things that bring **light** into the world.*

23 Thursday

READ
Acts 24

6:00

7:00

8:00

9:00

10:00

11:00

12:00

1:00

2:00

3:00

4:00

5:00

6:00

7:00

8:00

9:00

10:00

24 Friday

READ
Acts 25

6:00

7:00

8:00

9:00

10:00

11:00

12:00

1:00

2:00

3:00

4:00

5:00

6:00

7:00

8:00

9:00

10:00

25 Saturday

READ
Acts 26

6:00

7:00

8:00

9:00

10:00

11:00

12:00

1:00

2:00

3:00

4:00

5:00

6:00

7:00

8:00

9:00

10:00

What do you need to pray about this week?

To Do

Things you're thankful for this week:

26 Sunday

READe

Acts 27:1-26

6:00

7:00

8:00

9:00

10:00

11:00

12:00

1:00

2:00

3:00

4:00

5:00

6:00

7:00

8:00

9:00

10:00

27 Monday

READ

Acts 27:27-44

6:00

7:00

8:00

9:00

10:00

11:00

12:00

1:00

2:00

3:00

4:00

5:00

6:00

7:00

8:00

9:00

10:00

28 Tuesday

READ

Acts 28

6:00

7:00

8:00

9:00

10:00

11:00

12:00

1:00

2:00

3:00

4:00

5:00

6:00

7:00

8:00

9:00

10:00

29 Wednesday

READ

Romans 1

6:00

7:00

8:00

9:00

10:00

11:00

12:00

1:00

2:00

3:00

4:00

5:00

6:00

7:00

8:00

9:00

10:00

Jesus didn't keep a planner, but we do know how he spent his time: growing relationships with his friends. When Jesus visited Martha and Mary, Martha was upset that Mary didn't help in the kitchen. But Jesus said Mary chose the one thing that mattered most: spending time with him.

30 Thursday	31 Friday	1 Saturday	What do you need to pray about this week?
READ Romans 2	READ Romans 3	READ Romans 4	
6:00	6:00	6:00	
7:00	7:00	7:00	
8:00	8:00	8:00	
9:00	9:00	9:00	
10:00	10:00	10:00	
11:00	11:00	11:00	
12:00	12:00	12:00	
1:00	1:00	1:00	
2:00	2:00	2:00	
3:00	3:00	3:00	*To Do*
4:00	4:00	4:00	
5:00	5:00	5:00	
6:00	6:00	6:00	
7:00	7:00	7:00	
8:00	8:00	8:00	
9:00	9:00	9:00	
10:00	10:00	10:00	

Things you're thankful for this week:

Review your gratitude notes from the previous weeks, and write a prayer to Jesus thanking him for this month.

What experiences, insights, and moments kept you centered on Jesus this month? Record them here so you don't forget them.

Reviewing the previous month, how have you grown?

What is an area or two in which you'd like to continue to grow?

Review your appointments and tasks for the coming month. How are they aligned with Jesus' command to love others? Is there anything you need to cancel, add, or change? Pray about it; then update your schedule as needed.

Now write a prayer thanking Jesus for the month ahead, and include one way you're planning to stay focused on him.

To Do

Notes

Sunday	Monday	Tuesday
26	27	28
2	3	4
9	10	11
16	17	18
23	24	25
30	31	1

This month, focus on Jesus by...

Wednesday	Thursday	Friday	Saturday
29	30	31	1
5	6	7	8
12	13	14	15
19	20	21	22
26	27	28	29
2	3	4	5

Loving others: Who are you going to be intentional about showing love to this month? Write their names here, and schedule time to connect with them.

2 Sunday

READ
Romans 5

6:00

7:00

8:00

9:00

10:00

11:00

12:00

1:00

2:00

3:00

4:00

5:00

6:00

7:00

8:00

9:00

10:00

3 Monday

READ
Romans 6

6:00

7:00

8:00

9:00

10:00

11:00

12:00

1:00

2:00

3:00

4:00

5:00

6:00

7:00

8:00

9:00

10:00

4 Tuesday

READ
Romans 7

6:00

7:00

8:00

9:00

10:00

11:00

12:00

1:00

2:00

3:00

4:00

5:00

6:00

7:00

8:00

9:00

10:00

5 Wednesday

READ
Romans 8:1-21

6:00

7:00

8:00

9:00

10:00

11:00

12:00

1:00

2:00

3:00

4:00

5:00

6:00

7:00

8:00

9:00

10:00

We've said it before, but it's worth repeating: You cannot be Jesus-centered without loving others. Love is the fruit of being attached to the Vine. Use a highlighter to mark all your appointments this week that involve you loving others. Do you need to schedule more time for producing spiritual fruit?

6 Thursday	7 Friday	8 Saturday	What do you need to pray about this week?
READ *Romans 8:22-39*	READ *Romans 9:1-15*	READ *Romans 9:16-33*	

6 Thursday
READ
Romans 8:22-39

6:00

7:00

8:00

9:00

10:00

11:00

12:00

1:00

2:00

3:00

4:00

5:00

6:00

7:00

8:00

9:00

10:00

7 Friday
READ
Romans 9:1-15

6:00

7:00

8:00

9:00

10:00

11:00

12:00

1:00

2:00

3:00

4:00

5:00

6:00

7:00

8:00

9:00

10:00

8 Saturday
READ
Romans 9:16-33

6:00

7:00

8:00

9:00

10:00

11:00

12:00

1:00

2:00

3:00

4:00

5:00

6:00

7:00

8:00

9:00

10:00

What do you need to pray about this week?

To Do

Things you're thankful for this week:

9 Sunday	10 Monday	11 Tuesday	12 Wednesday
READ	READ	READ	READ
Romans 10	Romans 11:1-18	Romans 11:19-36	Romans 12
6:00	6:00	6:00	6:00
7:00	7:00	7:00	7:00
8:00	8:00	8:00	8:00
9:00	9:00	9:00	9:00
10:00	10:00	10:00	10:00
11:00	11:00	11:00	11:00
12:00	12:00	12:00	12:00
1:00	1:00	1:00	1:00
2:00	2:00	2:00	2:00
3:00	3:00	3:00	3:00
4:00	4:00	4:00	4:00
5:00	5:00	5:00	5:00
6:00	6:00	6:00	6:00
7:00	7:00	7:00	7:00
8:00	8:00	8:00	8:00
9:00	9:00	9:00	9:00
10:00	10:00	10:00	10:00

Jesus told his followers to be like a shining light to the world. In other words, the kind and good things they do will help people see God's goodness. As you look at your week ahead, what's one way you'll be shining the light of Jesus to those around you?

13 Thursday

READ
Romans 13

6:00

7:00

8:00

9:00

10:00

11:00

12:00

1:00

2:00

3:00

4:00

5:00

6:00

7:00

8:00

9:00

10:00

14 Friday

READ
Romans 14

6:00

7:00

8:00

9:00

10:00

11:00

12:00

1:00

2:00

3:00

4:00

5:00

6:00

7:00

8:00

9:00

10:00

15 Saturday

READ
Romans 15:1-13

6:00

7:00

8:00

9:00

10:00

11:00

12:00

1:00

2:00

3:00

4:00

5:00

6:00

7:00

8:00

9:00

10:00

What do you need to pray about this week?

To Do

Things you're thankful for this week:

16 Sunday	17 Monday	18 Tuesday	19 Wednesday
READ	READ	READ	READ
Romans 15:14-33	*Romans 16*	*1 Corinthians 1*	*1 Corinthians 2*
6:00	6:00	6:00	6:00
7:00	7:00	7:00	7:00
8:00	8:00	8:00	8:00
9:00	9:00	9:00	9:00
10:00	10:00	10:00	10:00
11:00	11:00	11:00	11:00
12:00	12:00	12:00	12:00
1:00	1:00	1:00	1:00
2:00	2:00	2:00	2:00
3:00	3:00	3:00	3:00
4:00	4:00	4:00	4:00
5:00	5:00	5:00	5:00
6:00	6:00	6:00	6:00
7:00	7:00	7:00	7:00
8:00	8:00	8:00	8:00
9:00	9:00	9:00	9:00
10:00	10:00	10:00	10:00

Focusing on Jesus doesn't mean ignoring everything—or everyone—else. It's quite the opposite. Jesus' command to love others means going out of your way to bring kindness, light, and grace into the lives of the people in your orbit. Take a moment to ensure you're focusing on that this week.

20 Thursday	21 Friday	22 Saturday	What do you need to pray about this week?
READ	READ	READ	
1 Corinthians 3	1 Corinthians 4	1 Corinthians 5	
6:00	6:00	6:00	
7:00	7:00	7:00	
8:00	8:00	8:00	
9:00	9:00	9:00	
10:00	10:00	10:00	
11:00	11:00	11:00	
12:00	12:00	12:00	
1:00	1:00	1:00	
2:00	2:00	2:00	
3:00	3:00	3:00	To Do
4:00	4:00	4:00	
5:00	5:00	5:00	
6:00	6:00	6:00	
7:00	7:00	7:00	
8:00	8:00	8:00	
9:00	9:00	9:00	
10:00	10:00	10:00	

Things you're thankful for this week:

23 Sunday

READ
1 Corinthians 6

6:00

7:00

8:00

9:00

10:00

11:00

12:00

1:00

2:00

3:00

4:00

5:00

6:00

7:00

8:00

9:00

10:00

24 Monday

READ
1 Corinthians 7:1-19

6:00

7:00

8:00

9:00

10:00

11:00

12:00

1:00

2:00

3:00

4:00

5:00

6:00

7:00

8:00

9:00

10:00

25 Tuesday

READ
1 Corinthians 7:20-40

6:00

7:00

8:00

9:00

10:00

11:00

12:00

1:00

2:00

3:00

4:00

5:00

6:00

7:00

8:00

9:00

10:00

26 Wednesday

READ
1 Corinthians 8

6:00

7:00

8:00

9:00

10:00

11:00

12:00

1:00

2:00

3:00

4:00

5:00

6:00

7:00

8:00

9:00

10:00

Draw a picture of a chair on two or three appointments on your calendar. As you spend time at those appointments, picture Jesus sitting with you in an empty chair in those spaces. What's it like having Jesus with you wherever you go?

27 Thursday

READt
1 Corinthians 9

6:00

7:00

8:00

9:00

10:00

11:00

12:00

1:00

2:00

3:00

4:00

5:00

6:00

7:00

8:00

9:00

10:00

28 Friday

READ
1 Corinthians 10:1-18

6:00

7:00

8:00

9:00

10:00

11:00

12:00

1:00

2:00

3:00

4:00

5:00

6:00

7:00

8:00

9:00

10:00

29 Saturday

READ
1 Corinthians 10:19-33

6:00

7:00

8:00

9:00

10:00

11:00

12:00

1:00

2:00

3:00

4:00

5:00

6:00

7:00

8:00

9:00

10:00

What do you need to pray about this week?

To Do

Things you're thankful for this week:

Review your gratitude notes from the previous weeks, and write a prayer to Jesus thanking him for this month.

_____

_____

_____

_____

_____

_____

_____

_____

_____

_____

_____

_____

_____

What experiences, insights, and moments kept you centered on Jesus this month? Record them here so you don't forget them.

_____

_____

_____

_____

_____

_____

_____

_____

_____

_____

_____

_____

_____

_____

_____

_____

Reviewing the previous month, how have you grown?

What is an area or two in which you'd like to continue to grow?

Review your appointments and tasks for the coming month. How are they aligned with Jesus' command to love others? Is there anything you need to cancel, add, or change? Pray about it; then update your schedule as needed.

Now write a prayer thanking Jesus for the month ahead, and include one way you're planning to stay focused on him.

SEPTEMBER 2020

Sunday	Monday	Tuesday
30	31	1
6	7 Labor Day	8
13	14	15
20	21	22
27	28	29

Notes

This month, focus on Jesus by...

Wednesday	Thursday	Friday	Saturday
2	3	4	5
9	10	11	12
16	17	18	19
23	24	25	26
30	1	2	3

Loving others: Who are you going to be intentional about showing love to this month? Write their names here, and schedule time to connect with them.

30 Sunday
READ
1 Corinthians 11:1-16

| 6:00 |
| 7:00 |
| 8:00 |
| 9:00 |
| 10:00 |
| 11:00 |
| 12:00 |
| 1:00 |
| 2:00 |
| 3:00 |
| 4:00 |
| 5:00 |
| 6:00 |
| 7:00 |
| 8:00 |
| 9:00 |
| 10:00 |

31 Monday
READ
1 Corinthians 11:17-34

| 6:00 |
| 7:00 |
| 8:00 |
| 9:00 |
| 10:00 |
| 11:00 |
| 12:00 |
| 1:00 |
| 2:00 |
| 3:00 |
| 4:00 |
| 5:00 |
| 6:00 |
| 7:00 |
| 8:00 |
| 9:00 |
| 10:00 |

1 Tuesday
READ
1 Corinthians 12

| 6:00 |
| 7:00 |
| 8:00 |
| 9:00 |
| 10:00 |
| 11:00 |
| 12:00 |
| 1:00 |
| 2:00 |
| 3:00 |
| 4:00 |
| 5:00 |
| 6:00 |
| 7:00 |
| 8:00 |
| 9:00 |
| 10:00 |

2 Wednesday
READ
1 Corinthians 13

| 6:00 |
| 7:00 |
| 8:00 |
| 9:00 |
| 10:00 |
| 11:00 |
| 12:00 |
| 1:00 |
| 2:00 |
| 3:00 |
| 4:00 |
| 5:00 |
| 6:00 |
| 7:00 |
| 8:00 |
| 9:00 |
| 10:00 |

Jesus usually traveled with a small group of close friends. When he called them his friends, he performed an act of service by washing their feet. What's one way you could serve a friend this week? By showing your friends love, you're centering your life on Jesus.

3 Thursday

READ
1 Corinthians 14:1-20

6:00

7:00

8:00

9:00

10:00

11:00

12:00

1:00

2:00

3:00

4:00

5:00

6:00

7:00

8:00

9:00

10:00

4 Friday

READ
1 Corinthians 14:21-40

6:00

7:00

8:00

9:00

10:00

11:00

12:00

1:00

2:00

3:00

4:00

5:00

6:00

7:00

8:00

9:00

10:00

5 Saturday

READ
1 Corinthians 15:1-28

6:00

7:00

8:00

9:00

10:00

11:00

12:00

1:00

2:00

3:00

4:00

5:00

6:00

7:00

8:00

9:00

10:00

What do you need to pray about this week?

To Do

Things you're thankful for this week:

6 Sunday

READ
1 Corinthians 15:29-58

6:00

7:00

8:00

9:00

10:00

11:00

12:00

1:00

2:00

3:00

4:00

5:00

6:00

7:00

8:00

9:00

10:00

7 Monday

READ
1 Corinthians 16

6:00

7:00

8:00

9:00

10:00

11:00

12:00

1:00

2:00

3:00

4:00

5:00

6:00

7:00

8:00

9:00

10:00

8 Tuesday

READ
2 Corinthians 1

6:00

7:00

8:00

9:00

10:00

11:00

12:00

1:00

2:00

3:00

4:00

5:00

6:00

7:00

8:00

9:00

10:00

9 Wednesday

READ
2 Corinthians 2

6:00

7:00

8:00

9:00

10:00

11:00

12:00

1:00

2:00

3:00

4:00

5:00

6:00

7:00

8:00

9:00

10:00

Do you ever worry about your schedule? It's not unusual if you do. But Jesus had something to say about it: "Can all your worries add a single moment to your life?" (Luke 12:25). Your appointments this week are not the most important thing in the world. What is? Loving Jesus and loving others.

10 Thursday

READE
2 Corinthians 3

6:00

7:00

8:00

9:00

10:00

11:00

12:00

1:00

2:00

3:00

4:00

5:00

6:00

7:00

8:00

9:00

10:00

11 Friday

READ
2 Corinthians 4

6:00

7:00

8:00

9:00

10:00

11:00

12:00

1:00

2:00

3:00

4:00

5:00

6:00

7:00

8:00

9:00

10:00

12 Saturday

READ
2 Corinthians 5

6:00

7:00

8:00

9:00

10:00

11:00

12:00

1:00

2:00

3:00

4:00

5:00

6:00

7:00

8:00

9:00

10:00

What do you need to pray about this week?

To Do

Things you're thankful for this week:

13 Sunday

READ
2 Corinthians 6

6:00

7:00

8:00

9:00

10:00

11:00

12:00

1:00

2:00

3:00

4:00

5:00

6:00

7:00

8:00

9:00

10:00

14 Monday

READ
2 Corinthians 7

6:00

7:00

8:00

9:00

10:00

11:00

12:00

1:00

2:00

3:00

4:00

5:00

6:00

7:00

8:00

9:00

10:00

15 Tuesday

READ
2 Corinthians 8

6:00

7:00

8:00

9:00

10:00

11:00

12:00

1:00

2:00

3:00

4:00

5:00

6:00

7:00

8:00

9:00

10:00

16 Wednesday

READ
2 Corinthians 9

6:00

7:00

8:00

9:00

10:00

11:00

12:00

1:00

2:00

3:00

4:00

5:00

6:00

7:00

8:00

9:00

10:00

Jesus once asked his followers, "Who am I to you?" It's a fair question. Jesus' identity is of profound significance for anyone who claims to be his follower. So who is Jesus to you? The kind of relationship you have with Jesus will impact everything you think about Jesus, as well as the people in your life.

17 Thursday

READ
2 Corinthians 10

6:00

7:00

8:00

9:00

10:00

11:00

12:00

1:00

2:00

3:00

4:00

5:00

6:00

7:00

8:00

9:00

10:00

18 Friday

READ
2 Corinthians 11:1-15

6:00

7:00

8:00

9:00

10:00

11:00

12:00

1:00

2:00

3:00

4:00

5:00

6:00

7:00

8:00

9:00

10:00

19 Saturday

READ
2 Corinthians 11:16-33

6:00

7:00

8:00

9:00

10:00

11:00

12:00

1:00

2:00

3:00

4:00

5:00

6:00

7:00

8:00

9:00

10:00

What do you need to pray about this week?

To Do

Things you're thankful for this week:

20 Sunday

READ
2 Corinthians 12

6:00

7:00

8:00

9:00

10:00

11:00

12:00

1:00

2:00

3:00

4:00

5:00

6:00

7:00

8:00

9:00

10:00

21 Monday

READ
2 Corinthians 13

6:00

7:00

8:00

9:00

10:00

11:00

12:00

1:00

2:00

3:00

4:00

5:00

6:00

7:00

8:00

9:00

10:00

22 Tuesday

READ
Galatians 1

6:00

7:00

8:00

9:00

10:00

11:00

12:00

1:00

2:00

3:00

4:00

5:00

6:00

7:00

8:00

9:00

10:00

23 Wednesday

READ
Galatians 2

6:00

7:00

8:00

9:00

10:00

11:00

12:00

1:00

2:00

3:00

4:00

5:00

6:00

7:00

8:00

9:00

10:00

One of the easiest ways to love others—and stay centered on Jesus in the process—is to encourage people. A simple note or a kind word can turn a person's entire week around. Try to encourage at least one person every day this week.

24 Thursday

READ
Galatians 3

6:00

7:00

8:00

9:00

10:00

11:00

12:00

1:00

2:00

3:00

4:00

5:00

6:00

7:00

8:00

9:00

10:00

25 Friday

READ
Galatians 4

6:00

7:00

8:00

9:00

10:00

11:00

12:00

1:00

2:00

3:00

4:00

5:00

6:00

7:00

8:00

9:00

10:00

26 Saturday

READ
Galatians 5

6:00

7:00

8:00

9:00

10:00

11:00

12:00

1:00

2:00

3:00

4:00

5:00

6:00

7:00

8:00

9:00

10:00

What do you need to pray about this week?

To Do

Things you're thankful for this week:

Review your gratitude notes from the previous weeks, and write a prayer to Jesus thanking him for this month.

What experiences, insights, and moments kept you centered on Jesus this month? Record them here so you don't forget them.

Reviewing the previous month, how have you grown?

What is an area or two in which you'd like to continue to grow?

Review your appointments and tasks for the coming month. How are they aligned with Jesus' command to love others? Is there anything you need to cancel, add, or change? Pray about it; then update your schedule as needed.

Now write a prayer thanking Jesus for the month ahead, and include one way you're planning to stay focused on him.

Setting Jesus-Centered Goals, Fourth Quarter

Look to Jesus' example to guide you during your goal-setting.

Before committing to goals, spend 5 to 10 minutes writing or mapping a sketch of everything that's currently on your heart relating to your dreams and aspirations. Don't edit yourself; it's okay if this list includes your most personal desires or things that seem impossible. Be open and honest with yourself about where your heart is right now.

Now think about Jesus' command to love others. How are Jesus' words connected to your own dreams and aspirations? Pray about it. Challenge yourself to be open to what that really means for you. If staying attached to Jesus is all about loving others, how will that affect your goals? If needed, rework your goals here.

With Jesus' command in mind, prayerfully consider one to three goals you can set for yourself for this quarter.

QUARTERLY GOAL (OCTOBER, NOVEMBER, DECEMBER)

Achieving this goal is important to you because…

Achieving this goal is important to Jesus because…

ACTION STEPS needed to accomplish this goal…

If you've identified one or two other quarterly goals, write them here along with the reasons they're important and the action steps you'll take to achieve them.

To Do

Notes

OCTOBER 2020

Sunday	Monday	Tuesday
27	28	29
4	5	6
11	12	13
	Columbus Day	
18	19	20
25	26	27

This month, focus on Jesus by...

Wednesday	Thursday	Friday	Saturday
30	1	2	3
7	8	9	10
14	15	16	17
21	22	23	24
28	29	30	31 Halloween

Loving others: Who are you going to be intentional about showing love to this month? Write their names here, and schedule time to connect with them.

27 Sunday

READ
Galatians 6

6:00

7:00

8:00

9:00

10:00

11:00

12:00

1:00

2:00

3:00

4:00

5:00

6:00

7:00

8:00

9:00

10:00

28 Monday

READ
Ephesians 1

6:00

7:00

8:00

9:00

10:00

11:00

12:00

1:00

2:00

3:00

4:00

5:00

6:00

7:00

8:00

9:00

10:00

29 Tuesday

READ
Ephesians 2

6:00

7:00

8:00

9:00

10:00

11:00

12:00

1:00

2:00

3:00

4:00

5:00

6:00

7:00

8:00

9:00

10:00

30 Wednesday

READ
Ephesians 3

6:00

7:00

8:00

9:00

10:00

11:00

12:00

1:00

2:00

3:00

4:00

5:00

6:00

7:00

8:00

9:00

10:00

If you had to pick the most important appointment of your week, which one would it be? Consider this: Even the most important event in your schedule is not nearly as significant as staying centered on Jesus and loving others. (It's possible to do both at the same time.)

1 Thursday

READ
Ephesians 4

6:00

7:00

8:00

9:00

10:00

11:00

12:00

1:00

2:00

3:00

4:00

5:00

6:00

7:00

8:00

9:00

10:00

2 Friday

READ
Ephesians 5:1-16

6:00

7:00

8:00

9:00

10:00

11:00

12:00

1:00

2:00

3:00

4:00

5:00

6:00

7:00

8:00

9:00

10:00

3 Saturday

READ
Ephesians 5:17-33

6:00

7:00

8:00

9:00

10:00

11:00

12:00

1:00

2:00

3:00

4:00

5:00

6:00

7:00

8:00

9:00

10:00

What do you need to pray about this week?

To Do

Things you're thankful for this week:

4 Sunday

READ
Ephesians 6

6:00

7:00

8:00

9:00

10:00

11:00

12:00

1:00

2:00

3:00

4:00

5:00

6:00

7:00

8:00

9:00

10:00

5 Monday

READ
Philippians 1

6:00

7:00

8:00

9:00

10:00

11:00

12:00

1:00

2:00

3:00

4:00

5:00

6:00

7:00

8:00

9:00

10:00

6 Tuesday

READ
Philippians 2

6:00

7:00

8:00

9:00

10:00

11:00

12:00

1:00

2:00

3:00

4:00

5:00

6:00

7:00

8:00

9:00

10:00

7 Wednesday

READ
Philippians 3

6:00

7:00

8:00

9:00

10:00

11:00

12:00

1:00

2:00

3:00

4:00

5:00

6:00

7:00

8:00

9:00

10:00

What would you do with an extra hour this week? Better yet, what could you do to give someone else an extra hour this week? Consider how being Jesus-centered might drive you to answer those questions.

8 Thursday	9 Friday	10 Saturday	What do you need to pray about this week?
READ *Philippians 4*	READ *Colossians 1*	READ *Colossians 2*	

8 Thursday	9 Friday	10 Saturday
6:00	6:00	6:00
7:00	7:00	7:00
8:00	8:00	8:00
9:00	9:00	9:00
10:00	10:00	10:00
11:00	11:00	11:00
12:00	12:00	12:00
1:00	1:00	1:00
2:00	2:00	2:00
3:00	3:00	3:00
4:00	4:00	4:00
5:00	5:00	5:00
6:00	6:00	6:00
7:00	7:00	7:00
8:00	8:00	8:00
9:00	9:00	9:00
10:00	10:00	10:00

To Do

Things you're thankful for this week:

11 Sunday

READ
Colossians 3

| 6:00 |
| 7:00 |
| 8:00 |
| 9:00 |
| 10:00 |
| 11:00 |
| 12:00 |
| 1:00 |
| 2:00 |
| 3:00 |
| 4:00 |
| 5:00 |
| 6:00 |
| 7:00 |
| 8:00 |
| 9:00 |
| 10:00 |

12 Monday

READ
Colossians 4

| 6:00 |
| 7:00 |
| 8:00 |
| 9:00 |
| 10:00 |
| 11:00 |
| 12:00 |
| 1:00 |
| 2:00 |
| 3:00 |
| 4:00 |
| 5:00 |
| 6:00 |
| 7:00 |
| 8:00 |
| 9:00 |
| 10:00 |

13 Tuesday

READ
1 Thessalonians 1

| 6:00 |
| 7:00 |
| 8:00 |
| 9:00 |
| 10:00 |
| 11:00 |
| 12:00 |
| 1:00 |
| 2:00 |
| 3:00 |
| 4:00 |
| 5:00 |
| 6:00 |
| 7:00 |
| 8:00 |
| 9:00 |
| 10:00 |

14 Wednesday

READ
1 Thessalonians 2

| 6:00 |
| 7:00 |
| 8:00 |
| 9:00 |
| 10:00 |
| 11:00 |
| 12:00 |
| 1:00 |
| 2:00 |
| 3:00 |
| 4:00 |
| 5:00 |
| 6:00 |
| 7:00 |
| 8:00 |
| 9:00 |
| 10:00 |

Invite a friend to spend some time with you this week, especially someone you haven't connected with in a while. Give the gift of your presence to that friend. Be attentive. Be the Jesus-centered person God wants you to be.

15 Thursday

READ
1 Thessalonians 3

6:00

7:00

8:00

9:00

10:00

11:00

12:00

1:00

2:00

3:00

4:00

5:00

6:00

7:00

8:00

9:00

10:00

16 Friday

READ
1 Thessalonians 4

6:00

7:00

8:00

9:00

10:00

11:00

12:00

1:00

2:00

3:00

4:00

5:00

6:00

7:00

8:00

9:00

10:00

17 Saturday

READ
1 Thessalonians 5

6:00

7:00

8:00

9:00

10:00

11:00

12:00

1:00

2:00

3:00

4:00

5:00

6:00

7:00

8:00

9:00

10:00

What do you need to pray about this week?

To Do

Things you're thankful for this week:

18 Sunday

READ
2 Thessalonians 1

6:00

7:00

8:00

9:00

10:00

11:00

12:00

1:00

2:00

3:00

4:00

5:00

6:00

7:00

8:00

9:00

10:00

19 Monday

READ
2 Thessalonians 2

6:00

7:00

8:00

9:00

10:00

11:00

12:00

1:00

2:00

3:00

4:00

5:00

6:00

7:00

8:00

9:00

10:00

20 Tuesday

READ
2 Thessalonians 3

6:00

7:00

8:00

9:00

10:00

11:00

12:00

1:00

2:00

3:00

4:00

5:00

6:00

7:00

8:00

9:00

10:00

21 Wednesday

READ
1 Timothy 1

6:00

7:00

8:00

9:00

10:00

11:00

12:00

1:00

2:00

3:00

4:00

5:00

6:00

7:00

8:00

9:00

10:00

If Jesus spent an entire day with you this week, what would you do? Where would you go together? What would the two of you talk about? If you're a Jesus-centered person, Jesus is already with you wherever you go.

22 Thursday

READ
1 Timothy 2

6:00

7:00

8:00

9:00

10:00

11:00

12:00

1:00

2:00

3:00

4:00

5:00

6:00

7:00

8:00

9:00

10:00

23 Friday

READ
1 Timothy 3

6:00

7:00

8:00

9:00

10:00

11:00

12:00

1:00

2:00

3:00

4:00

5:00

6:00

7:00

8:00

9:00

10:00

24 Saturday

READ
1 Timothy 4

6:00

7:00

8:00

9:00

10:00

11:00

12:00

1:00

2:00

3:00

4:00

5:00

6:00

7:00

8:00

9:00

10:00

What do you need to pray about this week?

To Do

Things you're thankful for this week:

25 Sunday

READ
1 Timothy 5

6:00

7:00

8:00

9:00

10:00

11:00

12:00

1:00

2:00

3:00

4:00

5:00

6:00

7:00

8:00

9:00

10:00

26 Monday

READ
1 Timothy 6

6:00

7:00

8:00

9:00

10:00

11:00

12:00

1:00

2:00

3:00

4:00

5:00

6:00

7:00

8:00

9:00

10:00

27 Tuesday

READ
2 Timothy 1

6:00

7:00

8:00

9:00

10:00

11:00

12:00

1:00

2:00

3:00

4:00

5:00

6:00

7:00

8:00

9:00

10:00

28 Wednesday

READ
2 Timothy 2

6:00

7:00

8:00

9:00

10:00

11:00

12:00

1:00

2:00

3:00

4:00

5:00

6:00

7:00

8:00

9:00

10:00

Whether you schedule it or not, you'll probably spend some time on social media this week. How do your social-media interactions reflect the heart of Jesus? Are you combative or accusatory? Are you invisible or irrelevant? Are you showing love...or something else?

29 Thursday

READ
2 Timothy 3

6:00

7:00

8:00

9:00

10:00

11:00

12:00

1:00

2:00

3:00

4:00

5:00

6:00

7:00

8:00

9:00

10:00

30 Friday

READ
2 Timothy 4

6:00

7:00

8:00

9:00

10:00

11:00

12:00

1:00

2:00

3:00

4:00

5:00

6:00

7:00

8:00

9:00

10:00

31 Saturday

READ
Titus 1

6:00

7:00

8:00

9:00

10:00

11:00

12:00

1:00

2:00

3:00

4:00

5:00

6:00

7:00

8:00

9:00

10:00

What do you need to pray about this week?

To Do

Things you're thankful for this week:

Review your gratitude notes from the previous weeks, and write a prayer to Jesus thanking him for this month.

What experiences, insights, and moments kept you centered on Jesus this month? Record them here so you don't forget them.

Reviewing the previous month, how have you grown?

What is an area or two in which you'd like to continue to grow?

Review your appointments and tasks for the coming month. How are they aligned with Jesus' command to love others? Is there anything you need to cancel, add, or change? Pray about it; then update your schedule as needed.

Now write a prayer thanking Jesus for the month ahead, and include one way you're planning to stay focused on him.

To Do

_____
_____
_____
_____
_____
_____
_____
_____
_____
_____
_____
_____
_____
_____
_____

Notes

NOVEMBER 2020

Sunday	Monday	Tuesday
1	2	3
8	9	10
15	16	17
22	23	24
29	30	1

This month, focus on Jesus by...

_____
_____
_____
_____
_____
_____
_____
_____
_____
_____
_____

Wednesday	Thursday	Friday	Saturday
4	5	6	7
11 Veterans Day	12	13	14
18	19	20	21
25	26 Thanksgiving Day	27	28
2	3	4	5

Loving others: Who are you going to be intentional about showing love to this month? Write their names here, and schedule time to connect with them.

1 Sunday	2 Monday	3 Tuesday	4 Wednesday
READ	READ	READ	READ
Titus 2	*Titus 3*	*Philemon 1*	*Hebrews 1*
6:00	6:00	6:00	6:00
7:00	7:00	7:00	7:00
8:00	8:00	8:00	8:00
9:00	9:00	9:00	9:00
10:00	10:00	10:00	10:00
11:00	11:00	11:00	11:00
12:00	12:00	12:00	12:00
1:00	1:00	1:00	1:00
2:00	2:00	2:00	2:00
3:00	3:00	3:00	3:00
4:00	4:00	4:00	4:00
5:00	5:00	5:00	5:00
6:00	6:00	6:00	6:00
7:00	7:00	7:00	7:00
8:00	8:00	8:00	8:00
9:00	9:00	9:00	9:00
10:00	10:00	10:00	10:00

Some people tend to focus on one aspect of Jesus' behavior. They may reason, "Jesus was angry at the money-changers in the Temple, so I'm going to be angry just like Jesus!" But Jesus showed a variety of emotions and responses to the people around him. To be Jesus-centered is to be whole. Commit all your emotions and behaviors to Jesus this week.

5 Thursday

READ
Hebrews 2

6:00

7:00

8:00

9:00

10:00

11:00

12:00

1:00

2:00

3:00

4:00

5:00

6:00

7:00

8:00

9:00

10:00

6 Friday

READ
Hebrews 3

6:00

7:00

8:00

9:00

10:00

11:00

12:00

1:00

2:00

3:00

4:00

5:00

6:00

7:00

8:00

9:00

10:00

7 Saturday

READ
Hebrews 4

6:00

7:00

8:00

9:00

10:00

11:00

12:00

1:00

2:00

3:00

4:00

5:00

6:00

7:00

8:00

9:00

10:00

What do you need to pray about this week?

To Do

Things you're thankful for this week:

8 Sunday

READ
Hebrews 5

6:00

7:00

8:00

9:00

10:00

11:00

12:00

1:00

2:00

3:00

4:00

5:00

6:00

7:00

8:00

9:00

10:00

9 Monday

READ
Hebrews 6

6:00

7:00

8:00

9:00

10:00

11:00

12:00

1:00

2:00

3:00

4:00

5:00

6:00

7:00

8:00

9:00

10:00

10 Tuesday

READ
Hebrews 7

6:00

7:00

8:00

9:00

10:00

11:00

12:00

1:00

2:00

3:00

4:00

5:00

6:00

7:00

8:00

9:00

10:00

11 Wednesday

READ
Hebrews 8

6:00

7:00

8:00

9:00

10:00

11:00

12:00

1:00

2:00

3:00

4:00

5:00

6:00

7:00

8:00

9:00

10:00

A lot of people struggle with being "good enough" for Jesus. Being Jesus-centered may feel like an impossible aspiration for a host of reasons. But Jesus accepts you with an overabundance of grace. Accept Jesus' grace this week, even among your mistakes and imperfections.

12 Thursday	13 Friday	14 Saturday	What do you need to pray about this week?
READ *Hebrews 9*	READ *Hebrews 10:1-18*	READ *Hebrews 10:19-39*	
6:00	6:00	6:00	
7:00	7:00	7:00	
8:00	8:00	8:00	
9:00	9:00	9:00	
10:00	10:00	10:00	
11:00	11:00	11:00	
12:00	12:00	12:00	
1:00	1:00	1:00	
2:00	2:00	2:00	
3:00	3:00	3:00	*To Do*
4:00	4:00	4:00	
5:00	5:00	5:00	
6:00	6:00	6:00	
7:00	7:00	7:00	
8:00	8:00	8:00	
9:00	9:00	9:00	
10:00	10:00	10:00	

Things you're thankful for this week:

NOV 15 – NOV 21

15 Sunday	16 Monday	17 Tuesday	18 Wednesday
READ *Hebrews 11:1-19*	READ *Hebrews 11:20-40*	READ *Hebrews 12*	READ *Hebrews 13*
6:00	6:00	6:00	6:00
7:00	7:00	7:00	7:00
8:00	8:00	8:00	8:00
9:00	9:00	9:00	9:00
10:00	10:00	10:00	10:00
11:00	11:00	11:00	11:00
12:00	12:00	12:00	12:00
1:00	1:00	1:00	1:00
2:00	2:00	2:00	2:00
3:00	3:00	3:00	3:00
4:00	4:00	4:00	4:00
5:00	5:00	5:00	5:00
6:00	6:00	6:00	6:00
7:00	7:00	7:00	7:00
8:00	8:00	8:00	8:00
9:00	9:00	9:00	9:00
10:00	10:00	10:00	10:00

What do you love most about Jesus? His wisdom? His strength? His generosity? His forgiveness? Something else? Pick an attribute of Jesus that you want to develop more in yourself. Find at least short periods of time on your calendar this week to pray and meditate on that quality.

19 Thursday

READ
James 1

6:00

7:00

8:00

9:00

10:00

11:00

12:00

1:00

2:00

3:00

4:00

5:00

6:00

7:00

8:00

9:00

10:00

20 Friday

READ
James 2

6:00

7:00

8:00

9:00

10:00

11:00

12:00

1:00

2:00

3:00

4:00

5:00

6:00

7:00

8:00

9:00

10:00

21 Saturday

READ
James 3

6:00

7:00

8:00

9:00

10:00

11:00

12:00

1:00

2:00

3:00

4:00

5:00

6:00

7:00

8:00

9:00

10:00

What do you need to pray about this week?

To Do

Things you're thankful for this week:

22 Sunday

READ
James 4

6:00

7:00

8:00

9:00

10:00

11:00

12:00

1:00

2:00

3:00

4:00

5:00

6:00

7:00

8:00

9:00

10:00

23 Monday

READ
James 5

6:00

7:00

8:00

9:00

10:00

11:00

12:00

1:00

2:00

3:00

4:00

5:00

6:00

7:00

8:00

9:00

10:00

24 Tuesday

READ
1 Peter 1

6:00

7:00

8:00

9:00

10:00

11:00

12:00

1:00

2:00

3:00

4:00

5:00

6:00

7:00

8:00

9:00

10:00

25 Wednesday

READ
1 Peter 2

6:00

7:00

8:00

9:00

10:00

11:00

12:00

1:00

2:00

3:00

4:00

5:00

6:00

7:00

8:00

9:00

10:00

Take a minute to review all your plans for this week. Is it a Jesus-centered week? You might look at your calendar and think you're seeing any number of "non-Jesus" activities. But don't be fooled into thinking like that. Jesus, and his command to love others, can be a part of everything you do.

26 Thursday	27 Friday	28 Saturday
READ	READ	READ
1 Peter 3	1 Peter 4	1 Peter 5
6:00	6:00	6:00
7:00	7:00	7:00
8:00	8:00	8:00
9:00	9:00	9:00
10:00	10:00	10:00
11:00	11:00	11:00
12:00	12:00	12:00
1:00	1:00	1:00
2:00	2:00	2:00
3:00	3:00	3:00
4:00	4:00	4:00
5:00	5:00	5:00
6:00	6:00	6:00
7:00	7:00	7:00
8:00	8:00	8:00
9:00	9:00	9:00
10:00	10:00	10:00

What do you need to pray about this week?

To Do

Things you're thankful for this week:

Review your gratitude notes from the previous weeks, and write a prayer to Jesus thanking him for this month.

What experiences, insights, and moments kept you centered on Jesus this month? Record them here so you don't forget them.

Reviewing the previous month, how have you grown?

What is an area or two in which you'd like to continue to grow?

Review your appointments and tasks for the coming month. How are they aligned with Jesus' command to love others? Is there anything you need to cancel, add, or change? Pray about it; then update your schedule as needed.

Now write a prayer thanking Jesus for the month ahead, and include one way you're planning to stay focused on him.

To Do

Notes

Sunday	Monday	Tuesday
29	30	1
6	7	8
13	14	15
20	21	22
27	28	29

This month, focus on Jesus by...

Wednesday	Thursday	Friday	Saturday
2	3	4	5
9	10	11	12
16	17	18	19
23	24 Christmas Eve	25 Christmas Day	26
30	31 New Year's Eve	1	2

Loving others: Who are you going to be intentional about showing love to this month? Write their names here, and schedule time to connect with them.

NOV 29 – DEC 5

29 Sunday	30 Monday	1 Tuesday	2 Wednesday
READ 2 Peter 1	READ 2 Peter 2	READ 2 Peter 3	READ 1 John 1
6:00	6:00	6:00	6:00
7:00	7:00	7:00	7:00
8:00	8:00	8:00	8:00
9:00	9:00	9:00	9:00
10:00	10:00	10:00	10:00
11:00	11:00	11:00	11:00
12:00	12:00	12:00	12:00
1:00	1:00	1:00	1:00
2:00	2:00	2:00	2:00
3:00	3:00	3:00	3:00
4:00	4:00	4:00	4:00
5:00	5:00	5:00	5:00
6:00	6:00	6:00	6:00
7:00	7:00	7:00	7:00
8:00	8:00	8:00	8:00
9:00	9:00	9:00	9:00
10:00	10:00	10:00	10:00

*Is Jesus invisible to you? It's safe to say that Jesus isn't literally sitting next to you right now in bodily form. But you **can** see Jesus...in the people all around you. As you love the people in your life, you're loving Jesus at the same time.*

3 Thursday

READ
1 John 2

6:00

7:00

8:00

9:00

10:00

11:00

12:00

1:00

2:00

3:00

4:00

5:00

6:00

7:00

8:00

9:00

10:00

4 Friday

READ
1 John 3

6:00

7:00

8:00

9:00

10:00

11:00

12:00

1:00

2:00

3:00

4:00

5:00

6:00

7:00

8:00

9:00

10:00

5 Saturday

READ
1 John 4

6:00

7:00

8:00

9:00

10:00

11:00

12:00

1:00

2:00

3:00

4:00

5:00

6:00

7:00

8:00

9:00

10:00

What do you need to pray about this week?

To Do

Things you're thankful for this week:

6 Sunday

READ
1 John 5

6:00

7:00

8:00

9:00

10:00

11:00

12:00

1:00

2:00

3:00

4:00

5:00

6:00

7:00

8:00

9:00

10:00

7 Monday

READ
2 John 1

6:00

7:00

8:00

9:00

10:00

11:00

12:00

1:00

2:00

3:00

4:00

5:00

6:00

7:00

8:00

9:00

10:00

8 Tuesday

READ
3 John 1

6:00

7:00

8:00

9:00

10:00

11:00

12:00

1:00

2:00

3:00

4:00

5:00

6:00

7:00

8:00

9:00

10:00

9 Wednesday

READ
Jude 1

6:00

7:00

8:00

9:00

10:00

11:00

12:00

1:00

2:00

3:00

4:00

5:00

6:00

7:00

8:00

9:00

10:00

Take a minute to describe one of your best friends. Focus on personality, not physical appearance. Write it down in two or three sentences. Now think about how you might describe Jesus to a friend. What's Jesus' personality like to you?

10 Thursday
READ
Revelation 1

6:00

7:00

8:00

9:00

10:00

11:00

12:00

1:00

2:00

3:00

4:00

5:00

6:00

7:00

8:00

9:00

10:00

11 Friday
READ
Revelation 2

6:00

7:00

8:00

9:00

10:00

11:00

12:00

1:00

2:00

3:00

4:00

5:00

6:00

7:00

8:00

9:00

10:00

12 Saturday
READ
Revelation 3

6:00

7:00

8:00

9:00

10:00

11:00

12:00

1:00

2:00

3:00

4:00

5:00

6:00

7:00

8:00

9:00

10:00

What do you need to pray about this week?

To Do

Things you're thankful for this week:

13 Sunday

READ
Revelation 4

6:00

7:00

8:00

9:00

10:00

11:00

12:00

1:00

2:00

3:00

4:00

5:00

6:00

7:00

8:00

9:00

10:00

14 Monday

READ
Revelation 5

6:00

7:00

8:00

9:00

10:00

11:00

12:00

1:00

2:00

3:00

4:00

5:00

6:00

7:00

8:00

9:00

10:00

15 Tuesday

READ
Revelation 6

6:00

7:00

8:00

9:00

10:00

11:00

12:00

1:00

2:00

3:00

4:00

5:00

6:00

7:00

8:00

9:00

10:00

16 Wednesday

READ
Revelation 7

6:00

7:00

8:00

9:00

10:00

11:00

12:00

1:00

2:00

3:00

4:00

5:00

6:00

7:00

8:00

9:00

10:00

What do you think Jesus loves most about you? There's definitely something, because Jesus most certainly loves you. Think about it, pray about it, and then write down what you imagine Jesus might tell you.

17 Thursday

READ
Revelation 8

6:00

7:00

8:00

9:00

10:00

11:00

12:00

1:00

2:00

3:00

4:00

5:00

6:00

7:00

8:00

9:00

10:00

18 Friday

READ
Revelation 9

6:00

7:00

8:00

9:00

10:00

11:00

12:00

1:00

2:00

3:00

4:00

5:00

6:00

7:00

8:00

9:00

10:00

19 Saturday

READ
Revelation 10

6:00

7:00

8:00

9:00

10:00

11:00

12:00

1:00

2:00

3:00

4:00

5:00

6:00

7:00

8:00

9:00

10:00

What do you need to pray about this week?

To Do

Things you're thankful for this week:

20 Sunday

READ
Revelation 11

6:00

7:00

8:00

9:00

10:00

11:00

12:00

1:00

2:00

3:00

4:00

5:00

6:00

7:00

8:00

9:00

10:00

21 Monday

READ
Revelation 12

6:00

7:00

8:00

9:00

10:00

11:00

12:00

1:00

2:00

3:00

4:00

5:00

6:00

7:00

8:00

9:00

10:00

22 Tuesday

READ
Revelation 13

6:00

7:00

8:00

9:00

10:00

11:00

12:00

1:00

2:00

3:00

4:00

5:00

6:00

7:00

8:00

9:00

10:00

23 Wednesday

READ
Revelation 14

6:00

7:00

8:00

9:00

10:00

11:00

12:00

1:00

2:00

3:00

4:00

5:00

6:00

7:00

8:00

9:00

10:00

Is your holiday season busy? Take a look at your schedule over the next week or two. What—or who—drives how you're going to spend your time? What role does Jesus play in your calendar during this time of the year?

24 Thursday	25 Friday	26 Saturday	What do you need to pray about this week?
READ *Revelation 15*	READ *Revelation 16*	READ *Revelation 17*	
6:00	6:00	6:00	--
7:00	7:00	7:00	--
8:00	8:00	8:00	--
9:00	9:00	9:00	--
10:00	10:00	10:00	--
11:00	11:00	11:00	--
12:00	12:00	12:00	--
1:00	1:00	1:00	--
2:00	2:00	2:00	--
3:00	3:00	3:00	*To Do*
4:00	4:00	4:00	--
5:00	5:00	5:00	--
6:00	6:00	6:00	--
7:00	7:00	7:00	--
8:00	8:00	8:00	--
9:00	9:00	9:00	--
10:00	10:00	10:00	--

Things you're thankful for this week:

27 Sunday	28 Monday	29 Tuesday	30 Wednesday
READ *Revelation 18*	READ *Revelation 19*	READ *Revelation 20*	READ *Revelation 21*
6:00	6:00	6:00	6:00
7:00	7:00	7:00	7:00
8:00	8:00	8:00	8:00
9:00	9:00	9:00	9:00
10:00	10:00	10:00	10:00
11:00	11:00	11:00	11:00
12:00	12:00	12:00	12:00
1:00	1:00	1:00	1:00
2:00	2:00	2:00	2:00
3:00	3:00	3:00	3:00
4:00	4:00	4:00	4:00
5:00	5:00	5:00	5:00
6:00	6:00	6:00	6:00
7:00	7:00	7:00	7:00
8:00	8:00	8:00	8:00
9:00	9:00	9:00	9:00
10:00	10:00	10:00	10:00

Is there anything you'd hoped to do this year but didn't? Would that thing have brought you closer to Jesus? Would that thing have given you an opportunity to show love to someone else? If so, make it a priority for next year. If not, think of something else that will definitely keep you centered on Jesus.

31 Thursday

READ
Revelation 22

6:00

7:00

8:00

9:00

10:00

11:00

12:00

1:00

2:00

3:00

4:00

5:00

6:00

7:00

8:00

9:00

10:00

1 Friday

READ
Matthew 1

6:00

7:00

8:00

9:00

10:00

11:00

12:00

1:00

2:00

3:00

4:00

5:00

6:00

7:00

8:00

9:00

10:00

2 Saturday

READ
Matthew 2

6:00

7:00

8:00

9:00

10:00

11:00

12:00

1:00

2:00

3:00

4:00

5:00

6:00

7:00

8:00

9:00

10:00

What do you need to pray about this week?

To Do

Things you're thankful for this week:

Review your gratitude notes from the previous weeks, and write a prayer to Jesus thanking him for this month.

What experiences, insights, and moments kept you centered on Jesus this month? Record them here so you don't forget them.

Reviewing the previous month, how have you grown?

What is an area or two in which you'd like to continue to grow?

Review your appointments and tasks for the coming month. How are they aligned with Jesus' command to love others? Is there anything you need to cancel, add, or change? Pray about it; then update your schedule as needed.

Now write a prayer thanking Jesus for the month ahead, and include one way you're planning to stay focused on him.